LEADERSHIP

2.0

TalentSmart®

11526 Sorrento Valley Road
San Diego, CA 92121

For information regarding special discounts for bulk purchases, contact TalentSmart® at:

888-818-SMART (toll free, US & Canada callers)
or 858-509-0582
Visit us on the web at www.TalentSmart.com

ISBN: 978-0-9743206-9-4
First Printing: 2012

Printed and assembled in the United States of America.

CONTENTS

1
LEADERSHIP 2.0

One of the most popular Dilbert comic strips in the cartoon's history begins with Dilbert's boss relaying senior leadership's explanation for the company's low profits. In response to his boss, Dilbert asks incredulously, "So they're saying that profits went up because of great leadership and down because of a weak economy?" To which Dilbert's boss replies, "These meetings will go faster if you stop putting things in context."

Great leadership is indeed a difficult thing to pin down and understand. You know a great leader when you're working for one, but even great leaders can have a hard time explaining the specifics of what they do that makes their leadership so effective. Great leadership is dynamic; it melds unique skills into an integrated whole.

The journey you're about to set off on will enable you to see leadership through a new lens and build valuable new skills into your leadership repertoire. The leadership skills explored in this book are the product of an intensive study that set out to separate the leadership skills that get results from those that are inconsequential or harmful. The first thing our study accomplished was pinpointing the 22 leadership skills critical to performance. Next, we looked closer at each skill and discovered that they all fall into one of two categories: the skills that get people into leadership positions in the first place and the skills that the greatest leaders use to rise above the rest. The first set of skills we deemed core leadership because together they form the basis of solid, productive leadership. The latter set of skills is called adaptive leadership because these skills create dynamic, agile leaders who are incredibly effective in any environment.

> **The leadership skills explored in this book are the product of an intensive study that set out to separate the leadership skills that get results from those that are inconsequential or harmful.**

Leadership 2.0 presents a new way to understand great leadership and an innovative method for any leader to become great. Core leadership will tighten your leadership game and make certain you have the building blocks in place to become an adaptive leader. The adaptive leadership skills will enable you to see and understand the specific actions the world's greatest leaders take every day. These things are not innate qualities of brilliant and inspirational people that you should aspire to—they are practical, repeatable skills that any leader can adopt with effort. We've broken down the core and adaptive leadership skills into straightforward components, supported by concrete strategies, so that you can apply them without unnecessary burden on your busy schedule.

> **The adaptive leadership skills will enable you to see and understand the specific actions the world's greatest leaders take every day.**

Core Leadership

Core leadership skills are the skills that get people promoted into leadership positions. People who naturally demonstrate these skills are often labeled "born" leaders. Core leadership skills are the foundation of effective leadership — they won't make you a great leader on their own, but you can't do it without them. Experienced leaders will recognize the core leadership section of this book as a great opportunity to sharpen the saw and take a new look at the skills they use every day. Aspiring leaders can learn the core leadership skills to mold their own blade.

CORE LEADERSHIP

STRATEGY	ACTION	RESULTS
Vision Acumen Planning Courage to Lead	Decision Making Communication Mobilizing Others	Risk Taking Results Focus Agility

CORE LEADERSHIP IS...

Strategy

Talent hits a target that no one else can hit, but genius hits a target no one else can see. Strategy is knowing how to look ahead, spot the trends, and anticipate the course of action you will follow to maximize your success.

Strategy requires:

Vision

Inspired leaders take their employees and the organization in new directions. This requires the ability to envision a new reality for others that they can see and want to pursue wholeheartedly.

Acumen

Savvy leaders possess an up-to-date understanding of the broader issues affecting their fields of expertise and their organizations.

Planning

Leaders must accurately anticipate upcoming events to set appropriate goals and get things done.

Courage to Lead
Courageous leaders stand strong in the face of adversity and take necessary risks to achieve results.

Action
An idea is a curious thing—it will not work unless you do. For most leaders, desire is not the factor that holds them back; it's knowing how to execute.

Action requires:

Decision Making
Effective leaders make sound decisions that consider multiple options, seek input from others where appropriate, and are reached in a timely manner.

Communication
When leaders create an open environment in which thoughts are expressed freely and information flows easily, they increase the effectiveness of their organization.

Mobilizing Others
Leaders must motivate and influence those around them. By mobilizing others, leaders move the organization as a whole toward obtainable and seemingly unobtainable results.

Results

It's a myth that hard work is enough to achieve results. Far too often, obstacles are thrown in a leader's path that require a special set of skills to reach the finish line.

Results require:

Risk Taking

Leaders must be able to maneuver through situations that require them to 'push the envelope,' risk their status in the organization, and stand behind a chosen course of action.

Results Focus

Leaders who achieve results stay focused, get and keep their people focused, and do whatever is necessary to see things through.

Agility

Leaders who consistently reach their goals are constantly adapting to their surroundings; they respond quickly to uncertainty and change to function effectively.

Adaptive Leadership

The adaptive leadership skills represent the major discovery from our research. That's not to suggest we "discovered" these skills. Rather, we found that adaptive leadership skills are what set great leaders apart—these skills represent the otherwise intangible qualities that great leaders have in common. Adaptive leadership is a unique combination of skills, perspective, and guided effort that enable true excellence. The adaptive leadership skills can take a leader at any level to places others cannot go. You just need a

> **Adaptive leadership is a unique combination of skills, perspective, and guided effort that enable true excellence.**

process to follow, and that's what Leadership 2.0 is all about.

ADAPTIVE LEADERSHIP

EMOTIONAL INTELLIGENCE	ORGANIZATIONAL JUSTICE
Self-Awareness Self-Management Social Awareness Relationship Management	Decision Fairness Information Sharing Outcome Concern

CHARACTER	DEVELOPMENT
Integrity Credibility Values Differences	Lifelong Learning Developing Others

ADAPTIVE LEADERSHIP IS...

Emotional Intelligence

Emotional intelligence is a set of skills that capture our awareness of our own emotions and the emotions of others and how we use this awareness to manage ourselves effectively and form quality relationships.

Emotional intelligence requires:

Self-awareness

The ability to accurately perceive your emotions in the moment and understand your tendencies across situations.

Self-management

Using awareness of your emotions to stay flexible and direct your behavior positively. This means managing your emotional reactions to situations and people.

Social Awareness

The ability to accurately pick up on other people's emotions and understand what is really going on with them.

Relationship Management

Using awareness of your emotions and those of others to manage interactions successfully.

Organizational Justice

Great leaders don't shy away from the truth. They know how to integrate what people think, what they want to hear, and how they want to hear it with the facts. This makes people feel respected and valued.

Organizational justice requires:

Decision Fairness
Leaders need to understand how people perceive fairness and then reach decisions through a fair process to increase the satisfaction, productivity, and retention of their employees.

Information Sharing
Once a decision has been made, employees must understand how the decision was reached and how specifically it impacts them.

Outcome Concern
A true leader is genuinely concerned with the welfare of others and is able to express this concern on a personal level with everyone he or she leads.

Character

Leaders who embody a true sense of character are transparent and forthcoming. They aren't perfect, but they earn people's respect by walking their talk.

Character requires:

Integrity
Integrity is the melding of ethics and values into action. Individuals who display this quality operate with a core set of beliefs that inspire admiration and support from others.

Credibility
Leaders who can be counted on and whose actions and opinions are sound gain the support and commitment of those around them.

Values Differences
Leaders who value and capitalize on the differences between people maximize their contributions and achieve better results.

Development

The moment leaders think they have nothing more to learn and have no obligation to help develop those they lead is the moment they ensure they'll never know their true potential.

Development requires:

Lifelong Learning
To stay on top of their game, effective leaders learn about themselves and their environment and use this knowledge to develop their abilities along many dimensions.

Developing Others
Leaders must provide their people with ample opportunities to grow and build new skills.

In addition to separating great leaders from the rest of the pack, adaptive leadership skills are what leaders overestimate their abilities in the most. We had leaders from a large cross section of industries rate themselves in all 22 core and adaptive leadership skills. We also had the leaders' peers, boss(es), and direct reports answer the same questions about them, and we compared the scores. As the table that follows illustrates, the five skills in which leaders overestimate their abilities the most are all adaptive leadership skills.

Top 5 Gaps* In Leaders' Awareness As Rated By:

Direct Reports	Peers	Boss(es)
1. Self-Awareness	1. Self-Awareness	1. Self-Awareness
2. Information Sharing	2. Information Sharing	2. Information Sharing
3. Social Awareness	3. Outcome Concern	3. Social Awareness
4. Outcome Concern	4. Developing Others	4. Values Differences
5. Developing Others	5. Social Awareness	5. Outcome Concern

* Leaders rated themselves higher than others did.

Contrary to what Dilbert might have us believe, leaders' gaps in self-awareness are rarely due to deceitful, Machiavellian motives or severe character deficits. In most cases, leaders—like everyone else—view themselves in a more favorable light than other people do. The fact that leaders' greatest overestimations are limited to the adaptive

> **The fact that leaders' greatest overestimations are limited to the adaptive leadership skills shows how tough these skills are to master and how few leaders have honed their skills adequately.**

leadership skills shows how tough these skills are to master and how few leaders have honed their skills adequately. As rare as adaptive leadership skills are, they present a perfect opportunity for leaders to get an edge and take their game to the next level.

360° Refined™

We want to help you make the best use of your time as you work to improve your leadership skills. A great way to do this is to take an objective look at where you stand in each of these 22 leadership skills before you begin working on them. To that end, there is a blue envelope in the back of this book that contains a passcode and instructions for you to go online and take the self-assessment portion* of the 360° Refined™ test. The 360° Refined™ test measures all 22 core and adaptive leadership skills, and you'll receive scores in each. It's the same test used in the study described on the previous page, and your results will give you a clear picture of how you stack up as a leader.

Each chapter of this book includes strategies to help you improve the skills addressed there. In addition to showing you which skills you should work on, your 360° Refined™ results include an analysis of your score profile to determine which strategies you should focus on to increase your leadership skills the most. The test's objectivity will help to increase your self-awareness, and the targeted results will ensure an efficient use of your time. You'll get an instant edge

---

* Your passcode to the self-assessment portion of 360° Refined™ does not include the ability to receive ratings from others. We apologize in advance, but please understand that 360° Refined™ sells for $300, and we cannot give the entire test away free with this book. If you'd like, you can unlock this feature for an additional fee (at a substantial discount).

when you discover where you have gaps in your leadership skills and what you can do to close those gaps.

Measuring your leadership skills takes your learning beyond a conceptual or motivational exercise—your score profile uncovers the skills you need to improve the most, and it pinpoints the individual strategies from this book that will help you get there. The value of measuring your leadership skills now is akin to learning the waltz with an actual partner. If we tell you how the dance works, you are likely to learn something and may even get the urge to try it yourself. If, as we show you how to do a waltz, you practice each step with a partner, your chances of remembering them later on the dance floor go up exponentially. The score profile you receive from taking 360° Refined™ is your dance partner in developing these skills. It will remind you where to step with every beat of the music.

Taking Action

Learning at the neural level moves along a continuum from having to concentrate hard on making a change to repeated polishing of the rough edges and finally to automatic habits that you hardly have to think about. The focus of your efforts at the outset ought to be on repeated practice for a period in a desired leadership skill—the same type of repeated practice an athlete endures until muscle memory takes over.

You should approach your practice of new leadership skills with the mindset of an athlete. Any day you walk into the office could be the most challenging day you've faced. Consider your workday your own personal gym that offers a variety of equipment for you to use to get your reps in. Every time you walk down the hall, into the boardroom, or into a staff meeting is an opportunity to hone your skills.

The Leadership 2.0 Action Plan that follows will help you focus your efforts effectively as you explore and apply the leadership skills in this book. There are six steps to completing your Leadership 2.0 Action Plan:

1. **Transfer your 360° Refined™ scores onto your Leadership 2.0 Action Plan.** Write down the leadership skills and behaviors that your test results

identified as your strengths and areas for improvement. This plan will serve as a valuable reference throughout your journey.

2. **Pick a leadership skill to work on.** When you're learning, your mind will focus best on one skill and the multiple behaviors that embody it. Even the most ambitious leader should trust that working diligently on a single skill ensures the most progress. Your feedback from 360° Refined™ points out the skill you should work on first. You may choose a different skill, but we recommend you choose something that will be visible to the people you work with and important to the organization your work for.

3. **Pick three behaviors you will commit to practicing for your chosen skill.** Feel free to choose from the lowest rated leadership behaviors in your 360° Refined™ report, the strategies from this book recommended for you based upon your 360° Refined™ score profile, or some of the other strategies from this book.

4. **Choose a leadership mentor.** Think about leaders you know who are gifted in your chosen leadership skill and ask one if he or she is willing to provide insight, feedback, and guidance in regular meetings.

5. Keep the following in mind as you practice your chosen leadership skill.

    a. Expect success, not perfection. Adopting new skills is a give-and-take process. Revel in small victories and don't expect yourself to get it right every time.

    b. Practice, practice, practice. You can't build muscle overnight, and the same is true for building new leadership skills. Solidifying the habits that will change who you are as a leader takes practice and repetition. Make certain to practice the actions you commit to as often as you can, with as many different people as you can.

    c. Be patient. Plan on it taking a month or two before you see significant progress in your leadership skills. Most people see measurable, enduring changes three to six months after they begin working on a new skill.

6. Repeat the process. Once you have a leadership skill mastered, it's time to pick another one and repeat the process. You can do this repeatedly until your leadership skills are where you need them to be.

If you haven't yet taken 360° Refined™, now is the time to do it. Once you're done reviewing your test results, begin exploring this book by completing the action plan that starts on the next page.

LEADERSHIP 2.0 ACTION PLAN

Date completed:

360° Refined ™ uses a frequency scale:

1 = Never, 2 = Rarely, 3 = Sometimes,

4 = Usually, 5 = Almost Always, 6 = Always

To summarize your leadership strengths, list your scores from 360° Refined™ below:

My Leadership Strengths

My five highest leadership skills:

Score   Skill

_____   _____

_____   _____

_____   _____

_____   _____

_____   _____

My five highest leadership behaviors:

Score   Leadership Behaviors

_____   1.

_____   2.

_____   3.

_____   4.

_____   5.

My Leadership Growth Areas

My five lowest leadership skills:

Score   Skill

_____   _____

_____   _____

_____   _____

_____   _____

_____   _____

My five lowest leadership behaviors:

Score   Leadership Behaviors

_____   1.

_____   2.

_____   3.

_____   4.

_____   5.

My Plan for Action

Based on the chapter that covers the skill that is your chosen leadership growth area, list three actions below that you will take to increase your impact as a leader.

1.

2.

3.

My Leadership Mentor

Whom do you know who is gifted in your chosen leadership skill and willing to provide feedback and advice throughout your efforts to improve?

My leadership mentor is:

CORE LEADERSHIP

2
STRATEGY

People tend to think of strategic leaders as 'trust your gut' types who make mysterious moves when the mood strikes them, but the creativity and insight that drive sound strategic thinking follow a careful and deliberate process. Effective strategies are the product of four unique leadership skills: vision, acumen, planning, and the courage to lead. When used in concert, these skills can change an industry landscape as easily as they can change the face of a company.

Consider the strategy behind Apple's release of the iPod back in the fall of 2001. Apple was far from the first to market—other portable music players had been commercially available for years—but by 2004 Apple had gained market share in excess of 70%. Apple took their time releasing the iPod because they recognized that digital music players were still an emerging technology and the right product could quickly gain market share. Few people— Apple's competitors included—would have guessed what a bomb Apple was about to drop on the industry. But the folks at Apple knew full well what they were doing. Apple's strategy coupled great technology with a sustainable and highly profitable business model. Before the product was even released, leaders at Apple could articulate why the product itself would warrant market share and how they had the tools in place to deliver and build momentum for the product in the marketplace. It took vision, acumen, planning, and ultimately courage to pull this off—the four skills that together make for a sound strategy. To be effective as a leader, you must have the vision to see beyond your competition, the acumen and planning to implement your vision, and the courage to stand your ground in the face of doubt or criticism.

Vision

A solid vision creates an idealized future state for your organization that everyone is motivated to pursue wholeheartedly. A vision ensures people don't just understand where the organization is headed, they understand *why* it's moving in the stated direction, and they want to do everything they can to help it get there. A vision sets a clear direction for the

> You want your vision to change the way people see their work—it should motivate all to act without self-interest in the pursuit of a superordinate goal.

entire organization, it generates spontaneous energy and enthusiasm, and it simplifies work by aligning everyone's efforts. You want your vision to change the way people see their work—it should motivate all to act without self-interest in the pursuit of a superordinate goal.

Vision and mission statements are common in organizations these days. Unfortunately, many of them do little more than hang on the wall in the lobby for visitors to read while they are waiting for their meeting. Too many leaders miss that the purpose of a vision is to create a direction for the organization that people can believe in. A vision is not about words on a wall. It is about creating a central pursuit for the organization that gives employees a sense of purpose. People operate at full capacity when they are energetically hunting an important objective.

The strategies that follow will help you to create a clear and compelling vision for your people.

1. Give Them a Purpose

You will know when your vision is well executed because you will see that people believe in it. A vision that people can believe in makes it easy for them to love their jobs. It creates a sense of

...people will work hard for a paycheck, and even harder for a person, but they'll work the hardest for a purpose.

community through a shared sense of purpose. After all, people will work hard for a paycheck, and even harder for a person, but they'll work the hardest for a purpose.

2. Don't Confuse Values with Vision

Don't mistake an esoteric list of values (teamwork, excellence, and the like) for vision. Values are important and have their place in business, but they are too vague to be an effective part of your vision.

3. Give Them Something to Talk About

A vision does not need to be written down to impact an organization's culture and the experience of employees. It needs to be shared. Don't confuse distribution with buy-in. The moment you assume your vision will impact employees' work is the moment you fail.

Since a vision needs to be communicated, you'll have to come up with something that people can easily share with one another. Your vision must balance being realistic and feasible with being audacious enough to drive people and get them to let go of their routines. It should be brief enough to be easily communicated, yet detailed enough that people know exactly what they're after. Your vision will not generate the contagious enthusiasm needed for execution if you expect people to pass it around in a tabbed binder.

4. Create Freedom

A well-executed vision requires you to relinquish control and trust others to execute the path you've laid out for them. You have to give your people the freedom to do their jobs in pursuit of the vision. If you don't have faith in their ability to execute it—and fall into the trap of micromanaging their work or being an authoritarian dictator that rules with a heavy hand—you will not see your vision realized.

5. Test Your Vision

You'll know your vision is complete when you can answer all of the following questions in the affirmative:

i. **Is my vision easy for other people to see?**
Your vision needs to be as clear to everyone else as it is inside your head.

ii. **Does my vision stimulate their interest and get their juices flowing?**
The energy your vision creates should be palpable. If people aren't bubbling with excitement at the prospect of the future you've laid out, you haven't done your job.

iii. **Does my vision get people moving spontaneously?**
Waiting for marching orders is not the same as rushing off to battle. Your vision should be so clear that people can and will pursue it without guidance.

iv. Is my vision realistic?

Your vision must be something your organization can realistically execute. You don't want your people chasing a pipe dream.

v. Is my vision so clear that people can spread the word?

Word-of-mouth contagion is one of the main keys to a successful vision. Think about some of the previous questions: if people are bubbling with excitement and moving spontaneously, then they are going to spread the word. Your vision has to be clear enough to enable them to do so.

vi. Would everyone continue to pursue this vision even in my absence?

Don't make your vision about you. If your vision is truly about the greater good of the organization, they will pursue it with or without you.

Once you can answer all of these questions with a yes, you're ready to move on and begin working to ensure you have the acumen, planning, and courage to lead to see your vision through.

What Vision Looks Like

Ted B.
Vision score = 6*

What people who work with him say:
"Ted is a very strong visionary. He has the ability to conceptualize a future state and assemble all the pieces necessary to get there, even if the journey is a long and complex one."

"Ted has that rare talent for seeing the big picture and knowing where a brand should grow to. He is passionate about his team and its work and is great at creating passion for the vision and moving toward it."

"He's great at casting vision. He understands where the company is going, envisions a better way of doing things, formulates a plan of action, and considers the impact on all areas of the operation."

"He sees possibilities in circumstances that others miss. He sees the value of stretching 'traditional' thinking in order to reach more people. He is willing to look at the current model we are using and to tweak and change it where necessary in order for us to be more effective."

* Scores are on the 1- to 6-point scale (1=never and 6=always) from the 360° Refined™ test. Scores represent the average rating received from all who rated the executive. Scores and coworker comments are from actual people, though names and other identifying information have been altered.

Lana A.
Vision score = 5.8

What people who work with her say:

"Lana is an excellent leader and visionary. She has an exceptional ability to clearly articulate and express her vision and ideas to executive leaders or lower level staff."

"Lana's dominant skill is leadership. She is a natural leader to whom others gravitate. No matter how bad the situation (e.g., depths of last fiscal year), she sees the path to a better future. This leads to a second strength, that of vision. She is a forward thinker who constantly innovates. She helps her team see the full extent of possibilities and gets them all on board to go there with her."

"Lana is a collaborator and partner across corporate. She takes on projects that drive our 'One Company' theme and strives to include the complete picture whenever possible. She has found ways to build an integrated marketing function by herself and has grown the team to accommodate her vision for the department. This is no easy task at a company that had never had this function in its 100+ years. Lana has the unique ability to see the vision or end state of a project."

What a Lack of Vision Looks Like

Jan F.
Vision score = 2.3

What people who work with her say:

"Jan needs to provide clear vision and leadership about exactly how we should be dealing with various market shifts. Last year, she met with employees all over campus to gather information and discuss issues, concerns, and ideas for improvement, especially after layoffs had significantly affected the organization. She compiled and summarized all of that information and sent it directly to all employees as a report of the discussions, but provided very little direction or response to the issues raised. Many employees were left thinking it was great that we had an opportunity to hear that there were many shared concerns, but what next? One could speculate that responding to the issues was left to middle management, but there wasn't a clear top-down plan that would have helped managers to be consistent."

"Jan needs to create a vision that people can really sink their teeth into and get behind…be the inspiration that motivates people. She does not give off the impression that she is here for the long haul, and that doesn't inspire people to get behind her leadership. If she were to inspire people with a vision that everyone can get behind and feel like we are all a part of, she would have a lot more support."

Bo R.
Vision score = 1.6

What people who work with him say:

"At times I think Bo questions his own belief in what we are doing and where we are headed. He will need to believe in what we are doing in order to make it happen."

"Bo needs to shape the value he brings to the executive team meetings. He doesn't prepare for discussions that allow him to offer his insight on the future of the organization."

"He needs to help the company adapt. Bo has to help shape the future while continuing to maintain the revenue stream as the funding source for new ventures. He isn't thinking through how his executive team changes as the organization changes, nor what he can be doing to drive them to help us going forward."

Acumen

As a leader, you demonstrate acumen in knowing your business better than anyone else. Not on the ground floor, mind you. You need to be able to see your business from above. Your job as a leader is to take a 30,000-foot view of your organization and your industry, so that you can spot opportunities that will create real competitive advantage.

Your organization has many moving parts, and you must be fluent in each of them before you can develop acumen. Acumen moves beyond fluency to understanding how all facets of your organization work together. You aren't expected (or should aspire) to know each

> **Your job as a leader is to take a 30,000-foot view of your organization and your industry, so that you can spot opportunities that will create real competitive advantage.**

individual aspect of the business better than anyone else, you just need to be fluent enough in each area to understand the essential elements of the enterprise. You then combine your understanding of these elements from a broad perspective that enables you to see things no one else can.

Great leaders are every bit as practical as they are visionary. Practical knowledge is a reflection of your acumen—how well you understand your business and the environment in which it operates. You cannot develop sound strategies that your people will buy in to if you don't demonstrate a real understanding of your own enterprise.

Acumen also requires broad knowledge of your industry and, often, the world at large. External trends must be an integral component of your internal strategies. Some of the most important trends affecting any enterprise are those that cannot be isolated to your company or even your industry. Your ability to stay abreast of these trends and integrate them into your strategies through a refined knowledge of your enterprise is the essence of business acumen.

> **External trends must be an integral component of your internal strategies.**

As you challenge yourself to sharpen your level of acumen, ask yourself the following questions. Your answers will reveal the areas where you need to develop your acumen further.

1. What events are shaping the world at large?

2. What events are shaping our industry?

3. What events are shaping our company?

4. What significance do these events hold for us?

5. What pieces do we have in place to capitalize on these events?

6. What do we still need to capitalize on these events?

7. How will we do it?

Taking the time to complete this exercise by answering the questions above will help you to refine your thinking and fill any gaps in your acumen. It's important that you have an accurate understanding of the issues your business is facing and that you take the time to gather the answers (including speaking to individuals both inside and outside your organization) needed to keep your knowledge sharp. Increasing your acumen will help you to manage complexity and remain effectively decisive when faced with uncertainty and change. As long as you talk to the right people, stay abreast of important trends, and get your industry dialed, you'll be equipped to develop sound strategies that create real competitive advantage.

What Acumen Looks Like

Jeri-Ann S.
Acumen score = 5.8*

What people who work with her say:

"Jeri-Ann has a deep sense of business acumen. She knows innately what is important to her organization and to the company. She is great at aligning technology to achieve business goals. She's great at articulating business problems to technology teams and conversely can express technical challenges in layperson's terms to her business stakeholders."

"Jeri-Ann has a brilliant mind in that her capacity for creative thinking is nearly perfectly balanced by her expertise. She is great at observing a situation and quickly providing an alternative way of approaching it or solving a problem in an effective manner."

"Jeri-Ann's industry experience allows her to anticipate the needs of the organization. She has the expertise to oversee very high-level solutions and provide answers to the organization's needs. She has an easygoing way about her that is persuasive along with a high level of understanding that engenders cooperation from peers. She is an extremely knowledgeable and impressive person."

* Scores are on the 1- to 6-point scale (1=never and 6=always) from the 360° Refined™ test. Scores represent the average rating received from all who rated the executive. Scores and coworker comments are from actual people, though names and other identifying information have been altered.

Brett W.
Acumen score = 5.5

What people who work with him say:
"Brett understands all aspects of our business. And what he may not know as much about, he relies on us as managers to share our knowledge and expertise in our areas. This collaboration results in the best decisions for our company."

"Brett does not focus exclusively on his function's concerns, but on all aspects of the business. He understands and can communicate our tactical and strategic objectives about as well as anyone in the company. He has big picture knowledge of the entire business."

"Brett is strong in communication and business acumen. He works hard to learn as much as he can about each business unit, their business, customers, products, and needs so that he can alter the logistics strategies to better support them."

"Brett really understands how decisions can affect the entire company. There have been a few situations when I thought an idea of mine would work. Brett pointed out that while it would drive more sales, it would also result in more labor hours as well as more money on energy utilization. Brett encouraged me to rethink the idea."

What a Lack of Acumen Looks Like

Kameko T.
Acumen score = 2

What people who work with her say:
"Kameko needs to stay more focused on business objectives, clearly communicate the plan, and show progress against it. She doesn't demonstrate that she knows the business. She needs to see her time and value-add differently from how she is conceptualizing them now. She needs to take time out of her day to reflect and strategize about what the project needs. She should also define where key risks and gaps are, not just go after already-defined key risks and gaps. Sometimes I wonder how well Kameko understands how to operate a business like ours."

"It would help if Kameko expanded the definition of a project's success beyond meeting deadlines and staying within budget. It would be great to get her expertise and perspective focused on the larger strategic relevance of the scope we are taking on and how the team is working together and communicating."

"In today's economic environment, she needs to be better informed about the organization's fundamentals, increase her willingness to take risks, and challenge the status quo. For example, she discussed unrelated regulations during discussions at the Transformation Committee, not realizing she had them confused."

Jeff D.
Acumen score = 1.8

What people who work with him say:
"Jeff needs to better understand the business, what each unit is producing, how they are organized, and what hurdles they face. He should also get to know our four core industries better. He struggles with how we're organized and where we are located, more so than other vice presidents that were hired two years ago."

"Jeff understands his function very well, but he needs to bring a broader cross-business perspective to his role to help elevate the function. He also needs to better account for the implications of the changes he is making on the other businesses, and ensure that we have a holistic solution."

"There appears to be limited depth in his knowledge of the inner workings of a multinational company. I believe he has not gained the respect and trust of the organization. At several meetings, Jeff has discussed inconsequential topics. He would be better off listening and learning."

"Jeff can't really communicate the 'why' of his objective, the benefit of that objective, and how he will get there. The challenge is that without better business acumen, he could lose credibility when he starts talking to employees 'off the cuff' about business results."

Planning

Leaders that excel in executing their vision tend to be very skilled at planning. Planning is essential—it ensures your strategy is well thought-out and can be implemented successfully. Yet, careful planning is often overlooked because it's a grind. Make no mistake about it; failing to plan adequately is a recipe for disaster. Some of the biggest mistakes leaders make are the result of failing to ensure resources are adequate and strategies are feasible.

> **Some of the biggest mistakes leaders make are the result of failing to ensure resources are adequate and strategies are feasible.**

The seven planning strategies that follow will help you to reduce the likelihood of performance shortfalls in the execution of your strategies. Follow them carefully and you'll be equipped to handle the obstacles that stand in the way of reaching your goals.

1. Focus on the Big Picture

Your plans are designed to support your broader strategy. As you dive into the details of planning, it's easy to become myopic and lose sight of the bigger picture. At regular intervals during the planning process, you should check your progress against the broader perspective to make certain you aren't losing the forest for the trees.

2. Know the Players

To plan effectively you need to have an accurate understanding of the skill sets and capabilities of everyone who will work to execute your plans. Your accuracy in assessing the human capital at your disposal is one of the biggest indicators of the eventual success or failure of any plan.

3. Be Realistic

It's a lot more fun to plan ambitiously than it is to execute ambitious plans. There's nothing wrong with being zealous —just make sure your plans are realistic. Otherwise, you risk burning everyone out.

4. Grind It Out

As a corollary of being realistic, you will inevitably find moments when even the best-laid plans require some serious tenacity to execute. Be prepared for the inevitable grind, and be strategic about when to push hard to avoid burnout.

5. Don't Run Too Lean

It's tempting to lay out a plan that runs lean on staffing and resources because this creates efficiency, but this efficiency only exists on paper. It's better to have a larger budget and scope than you'll use, rather than create something that looks great on paper but ultimately fails.

6. Expect the Unexpected

Unexpected events can accelerate, alter, or derail your plans. You should eagerly await unexpected influences, rather than getting blindsided by them. Don't forget to incorporate Murphy's Law ("Anything that can go wrong, will") and its corollaries ("Everything takes longer than you think" and "Nothing is as easy as it looks") in your planning.

> **You should eagerly await unexpected influences, rather than getting blindsided by them.**

7. Set and Check Against Milestones

You need to set targets against which you can measure the success of your plans. Setting these targets is the easy part, particularly if you take the time to set them at the beginning of the planning process. It's more difficult, and absolutely necessary, to hold yourself accountable to them once you're working to execute your plans.

Planning may be one of the least fun activities a leader is responsible for, but it's no less important than anything else you do. Just remember, when you're trying to muster the motivation to take the time to plan, that every moment you spend planning will be absolutely worth it in the end.

What Planning Looks Like

Javier G.
Planning score = 6*

What people who work with him say:
"Javier is the master of planning and preparation. He is conscientious, dependable, and great with follow up and follow through. He should continue to use his great skills to lead initiatives in the future."

"Javier is great at laying out a plan and the process to rollout priorities in the most time- and cost-effective way. He is forward thinking and predicts possible issues that could arise and creates plans to be sure we know how to handle a situation before it happens. I know you can't account for everything that will come up in rolling out broad initiatives, but Javier will already have a plan laid out for most obstacles to be sure that we create the best quality outcome in the shortest amount of time."

"Javier excels at many things, but I believe he's best at planning initiatives, both large and small. He's able to see potential pitfalls and plan for minute details from his knowledge of technology and vast experience in the field. I can't think of a specific example offhand, but he can routinely spot trouble with a plan where others may not."

* Scores are on the 1- to 6-point scale (1=never and 6=always) from the 360° Refined™ test. Scores represent the average rating received from all who rated the executive. Scores and coworker comments are from actual people, though names and other identifying information have been altered.

Noreen G.
Planning score = 5.6

What people who work with her say:

"Noreen is great at planning and looking toward the future. She's proactive, which allows her to react when she needs to, not because she has to."

"Noreen is very adept at planning. She can take a complex business task, develop the necessary plan, allocate resources (both funding and people) effectively, schedule appropriately, monitor incrementally, and deliver on time and under budget every time."

"She is excellent in planning, organizing, and creating positive outcomes in everything she sets her mind to doing. She is ahead of the game at all times and it allows her to see opportunities and take them for the benefit of all. Her great work ethic spills over to those around her. I would say planning and implementing are her greatest strengths."

What a Lack of Planning Looks Like

Ashton D.
Planning score = 2

What people who work with him say:
"Ashton always seems to be behind the eight ball when it comes to planning, specifically sizing up problems and opportunities. He doesn't understand what all the elements are that are needed to come together to make it happen and when. This is where he should focus all his development efforts."

"Ashton needs to get ahead by planning better. If the devil is in the details, the devil is winning. He needs to be all about organization and attention to the smallest of details, and he is not leading the team in this area."

Saundra H.
Planning score = 1.7

What people who work with her say:
"Stop reacting to every issue and start planning ahead. Marketing functions are a cyclical process. There should be more stability. Also, please make more thought-out decisions. No one expects you to know everything right

on the spot. And don't say yes to every request without consulting key resources and ensuring commitments can be met."

"Saundra's time management skills need work. She does not understand what is important and what can be deferred. To her everything is critical, so she is often overwhelmed."

"Saundra misses deadlines, is late to meetings, and pulls all-nighters and other crazy things to pull off a deliverable. Then she takes credit for stomping out the fire when in fact she was the one who set it in the first place."

Courage to Lead

Aristotle wisely said that courage is the first virtue that makes all other virtues possible. This is especially true in leadership, where good strategies take courage to implement. Even if the strategy itself is not particularly bold or revolutionary, there are inevitable junctures in the implementation process that are bound to test your mettle. Leaders must have the courage to stand strong in these moments—to be decisive and choose a direction without fear of the blame that will come with the wrong course of action.

Extraordinary leaders demonstrate courage in the face of adversity. For the courageous leader adversity is a welcome test. Like a blacksmith's molding of a red-hot iron, adversity is a trial by fire that refines leaders and sharpens their game. Adversity emboldens courageous leaders and leaves them more committed to their strategic direction. Courageous leaders turn the negatives of adversity into positives as they move forward with a greater sense of purpose. Leaders who lack courage simply toe the company line. They follow the safest path—the path of least resistance—because they'd rather cover their backside than lead.

> ...adversity is a trial by fire that refines leaders and sharpens their game.

People will wait to see if a leader is courageous before they're willing to follow his or her lead. Once people see that a leader is willing to make difficult decisions, challenge the status quo, rise above adversity, take responsibility for his or her actions, and the like, they see that it's safe to follow. People need courage in their leaders. They need someone who can make difficult decisions and watch over them. They need a leader who will stay the course when things get tough. Courageous leaders make people feel safe and protected, and people are far more likely to show courage themselves when their leaders do the same.

Courage can be an easy thing to aspire to and a difficult thing to demonstrate in the moment. The 10 essential elements of leadership courage that follow will help you become a more courageous leader:

1. Courage isn't about bravado—it's about having the guts to stand behind decisions when you're the one that will take the fall.

2. Courage isn't the absence of fear. Courage is the ability to move forward in the face of fear.

3. Courage demands discipline and consistency. Its enemies are distraction and compromise.

4. Courage requires having a voice—a voice that addresses difficult subjects, delivers tough feedback, and shares dissenting opinions.

5. Courage means doing the right thing even when it is dangerous to do so.

6. Courage requires letting go and allowing people to do their jobs.

7. Courageous leaders don't make excuses—they apologize.

8. Courage takes risks that others are unwilling to attempt.

9. Courage addresses conflict head-on.

10. Courage challenges the status quo.

If you're not the type that runs toward the sound of gunfire, don't worry; courage is a core leadership skill that can be developed with focus and effort. Your courage is manifest in the decisions you make every single day. Every day, indeed every decision, provides a new opportunity to act courageously. Courage is a highly visible skill—your people will notice when you demonstrate it in small or large doses. Of course, the best thing about becoming more courageous is there are few things in life more liberating than facing your fears.

> **...there are few things in life more liberating than facing your fears.**

What Courage to Lead Looks Like

Thach N.
Courage to lead score = 6*

What people who work with him say:

"Thach has an incredible sense of ownership. He will always put a results-oriented approach ahead of personal politics and perception-based decision making. He is wonderfully unafraid to 'step out of the box' with a new approach in situations where the same methods are not generating results."

"Thach is genuinely dedicated to achieving the best for the organization. He is proactive in making results visible, whether positive or negative, and is selfless in that effort. Thach is fully engaged and not afraid to get dirty by bringing tough issues to the fore so that they can reach a resolution. Thach practices what he preaches."

"He is a natural leader and is not afraid to make his voice known. Thach speaks up and says what others should, but are afraid to. What is great about him is that he is a direct person who is not afraid of conflict. He addresses difficult situations with ease and in a professional manner."

* Scores are on the 1- to 6-point scale (1=never and 6=always) from the 360° Refined™ test. Scores represent the average rating received from all who rated the executive. Scores and coworker comments are from actual people, though names and other identifying information have been altered.

Penny K.
Courage to lead score = 5.7

What people who work with her say:

"Penny is a superior leader because she leads by example. She consistently works hard, is innovative, and isn't easily rattled. She's rarely blown off course. She is not scared of making a tough decision and then backing it even if it makes others upset. Nor is she afraid to challenge existing hierarchy when necessary."

"I admire her tenacity, her professionalism, her work ethic, and her sense of fair play. I am also grateful that she is usually the one who speaks out on behalf of the group when some of us do not have the clarity of thought or the courage to do so."

"Penny is willing to stand up for her staff, which inspires loyalty in her team. For example, she is willing to talk to the Board regarding the issues the executive team deemed important to consider."

What a Lack of Courage to Lead Looks Like

Howard D.
Courage to lead score = 2

What people who work with him say:

"Howard needs to be brave enough to speak his mind regardless of whether his decisions or words are popular or unpopular. He should not be afraid to 'offend' people for the sake of achieving company or department results."

"Howard needs to have his own ideas and rely less on others to help him make decisions he's capable of making on his own. Collaboration is great, but at times a leader needs to follow his or her own vision and convictions, even if it means being unpopular."

"He shouldn't avoid the hard things. He has a lot of talent and ability, but it won't amount to much unless he learns how to persevere in difficult situations. Howard would rather ignore difficult situations than handle them head on as a leader should."

Dawn M.
Courage to lead score = 1.7

What people who work with her say:

"What's holding Dawn back, in my opinion, is fear of failure and anxiety over whether she has made the right decision to the point where by the time she has made a decision, it is not her own. The following words come to mind when I think of Dawn: afraid, tentative, holding back, worried."

"What Dawn can do better is act like a real leader, understand the whole picture and each piece of her job, and have the courage to take necessary creative steps to help the people under her, instead of simply agreeing with what is coming down the chain."

"You can tell that she has a lot of underlying fear and a lot of her actions are led by this fear, possibly of losing relationships, so she tends to be a people-pleaser and sacrifice herself and her values to please others."

"Be unafraid to step out and take risks in putting forth ideas and providing feedback. She appears to be overly concerned with harmony and consensus, and steps back from expressing things that need to be said or from taking the lead in moving a situation or project forward."

3
ACTION

Thank goodness for people who practice what they preach. Leadership development consultants are students of how people operate inside organizations and use this knowledge to help companies manage their most valuable assets—their people. Consultants with great ideas soon find themselves running their own burgeoning companies. This places them in an interesting predicament. That is, will they practice what they preach? Sadly, some do not.

We have seen consultants make great things happen in their companies by applying their own techniques and principles. Ken Blanchard is a prime example. You have probably heard of Ken. He wrote an immensely popular book called The One Minute Manager. Ken is a big believer in empowering people. He gets people moving by building their commitment, not through fear of reprisal.

> He gets people moving by building their commitment, not through fear of reprisal.

Like the figureheads of most companies, Ken is a busy guy. He travels the world speaking to groups about effective leadership. Yet he finds the time every single day (and has for decades) to do a fascinating thing for his people—he leaves them a voicemail. Each day, Ken's voicemail is delivered to the entire company, and he doesn't make these calls just to chitchat or leave a 'rah-rah' message like "Have a super day!" Ken leaves these messages to let everyone know where he is, what he's up to, and what he's learning.

By making a daily call to his employees, Ken lets everyone know what's on the mind of the man who makes some of the biggest decisions affecting their organization. It's a simple thing, really, what Ken does, but it's important because it motivates action. Ken's actions represent the kind of effort it takes as a leader to connect with people and empower them to act on behalf of the organization. People won't perform until the organization feels like a common unit that everyone has a vested interest in, and often it's the little things that help to make this happen.

> **People won't perform until the organization feels like a common unit that everyone has a vested interest in, and often it's the little things that help to make this happen.**

It's not that all leaders should leave a daily voicemail for their employees. What's important is that you search for ways to connect with your people and empower them to act. This is a challenge for some leaders who fail to realize that people don't take action when they're told to—people take action when they're compelled to. Leaders who motivate people to take action often do so with creative (and sometimes counterintuitive) methods, but they all rely on three critical skills—decision making, communication, and mobilizing others.

Decision Making

Bad decisions are an unavoidable fact of life. Sometimes you're going to make great choices, and other times you're going to shoot yourself right in the foot. The key to making good decisions is taking full control of your decision-making process. You need to understand and replicate the process by which you make your best decisions. Otherwise, you're bound to let circumstances under your control force you into playing the wrong hand.

> You need to understand and replicate the process by which you make your best decisions. Otherwise, you're bound to let circumstances under your control force you into playing the wrong hand.

Your ability to make sound decisions time and time again is paramount to your success as a leader. Leaders rise through the ranks of organizations by making good choices that drive the company forward. It takes years of good decision making to reach the elevated status that you desire as a leader, and you can throw it all away with just one poor decision. This is an unfortunate reality of leadership: the more you are responsible for, the quicker you can run the organization into the ground.

As a leader, you are only as good as your last decision. This makes it absolutely essential that you have a decision-making process that controls risk and enables you to make the best decisions possible. You need a system that allows you to accurately process the barrage of information that makes decision making so challenging. Integrate the following methods into your decision-making repertoire,

> **As a leader, you are only as good as your last decision.**

and they'll help you eliminate distractions, focus on the right information, and make sound decisions that accelerate your performance as a leader.

1. Take Your Emotions Out of the Driver's Seat

It's incredibly difficult to separate fact from fiction when your emotions are running strong. This is tricky because a positive emotion (excitement, bliss, etc.) can be just as detrimental to your decisions as a negative one. Positive emotions leave you feeling like you walk on water. This sense that you can do no wrong leads to rash decisions and mistakes. Negative emotions (stress, anxiety, etc.) on the other hand can also lead to poor decisions if you allow them to go unchecked. If you don't learn to manage your emotions, they will make your decisions for you. And, rest assured, your emotions will make poor decisions.

2. Seek Counsel

Good advice is a scarce commodity, but only because people are resistant to sticking their neck out to ask for it. Find your sounding board, and walk him or her through your decision-making process to gather feedback. Be thorough in explaining the situation, or the advice you receive will be shortsighted. Once you do receive advice, don't allow it to absolve you of your obligation. The final say must be your own.

3. Be Wary of Raw Data

Raw data is a source of bad decisions because it's easy to point at one stat or another to confirm what you already believe. Nothing makes people

Raw data is a source of bad decisions because it's easy to point at one stat or another to confirm what you already believe.

feel more confident in a bad decision than data that supports their inclination. What you want is information—an evolved data set in which the data has been carefully processed and integrated to create context and meaning. For example, you may have raw data on recent customer purchases that seems to suggest customers prefer a certain type of product, but when you analyze this data against purchase history, time of year, and purchase frequency, you discover that the customer interest in the product is momentary and insignificant (due to seasonal variations or other factors).

4. Seek Knowledge over Information

Whereas information is data that has been refined through analysis, knowledge is information that has been proven through testing and validation. Learn to recognize the difference in your data sources. It's far more effective to base your assumptions on knowledge that has been proven to solve important aspects of the problem you are grappling with. In the case of the customer data mentioned in the previous example, the data analysis that you received was information. Knowledge would come from

> **Whereas information is data that has been refined through analysis, knowledge is information that has been proven through testing and validation.**

testing this information against a new product release to see if the numbers hold up, or finding industry analysis that confirms the trend that you have witnessed.

5. Know What's Driving Your Inclination

Don't kid yourself when it comes to "the facts" that are powering your inclinations. When you're honest with yourself about what's driving you to lean one way or the other, you develop an objective perspective that allows you to remain flexible and incorporate new pieces of information without getting hung up on preexisting beliefs.

6. Consider Every Angle

Every important decision you make warrants careful analysis from every possible angle to ensure that you understand the potential repercussions of each course of action. The questions you should ask yourself include the following:

i. Why do I need to make this decision?

ii. What will happen if I don't make this decision?

iii. Who will be affected by this decision?

iv. How will this decision affect them?

v. What are the implications of each potential course of action?

Until you've answered all of these questions, you haven't even begun to look at your decision from every angle.

7. Do a Cost/Benefit Analysis

For every decision you make, you need to weigh the costs associated with each potential option against the potential benefits. Next, consider what will happen if your expected benefit falls short of your estimation and your costs exceed your estimation. Performing this analysis—especially the comparisons that factor in potentially inaccurate estimations on your part—will help you eliminate unsavory options whose risk outweighs the potential benefits.

8. Do an Integrity Gut Check

When considering potential options, ask yourself if each option is the right thing to do. You may be able to live with yourself, but would you still do it if you had to call your mother and explain the decision to her?

9. Prepare for Contingencies

No decision you make will proceed exactly as you planned. Prepare for contingencies ahead of time, so you won't be blindsided by unexpected consequences of your actions. You can't control every variable that will affect the ultimate

> **Prepare for contingencies ahead of time, so you won't be blindsided by unexpected consequences of your actions.**

success of your decisions, but you can control how you respond to contingencies. When the decisions you make are in response to industry and market trends, detailing potential consequences ahead of time is a great way to prepare yourself to act quickly and get a leg up on your competition.

As a leader, you will be watched closely in how you make decisions and how you respond to the consequences that result from the choices you've made. This necessitates expending extra effort to ensure you have a sound decision-making process. When you see the results that come from developing such a process, you'll realize it was worth every bit of your time, energy, and attention.

What Good Decision Making Looks Like

Thibaut H.
Decision-making score = 6*

What people who work with him say:

"Thibaut digs in to understand complex problems and breaks them down into fundamental elements that can be separately debated and resolved. He continuously learns from his experiences and strives to apply them, so his decisions and paths are well thought out and backed by a lot of data."

"He makes difficult decisions with a great deal of thought ahead of time. Being provided with background and facts that have contributed to the decisions being made gives me additional assurance not just in the decision being made but also in the process to arrive at the decision. I am confident that our company will do well under Thibaut's leadership."

"Thibaut asks many questions to gather as much information as possible before making a decision. I have worked with many leaders who jump to conclusions before finding the facts."

* Scores are on the 1- to 6-point scale (1=never and 6=always) from the 360° Refined™ test. Scores represent the average rating received from all who rated the executive. Scores and coworker comments are from actual people, though names and other identifying information have been altered.

Stephanie A.
Decision-making score = 5.7

What people who work with her say:
"She has the ability to see trends, analyze, and make appropriate, good decisions. She is firm about her decisions and flexible enough to make corrections immediately in order to obtain a goal."

"Stephanie is very effective at diagnosing a challenge or problem and prescribing the appropriate solution. She is very intuitive around process and equally good at dealing with strategic and tactical topics. She has a very sharp mind and is able to 'connect the dots,' and make decisions on the fly to drive success in difficult situations."

"Stephanie has an excellent capacity to see the overall picture and strives to make decisions on the whole issue rather than bits and pieces. She takes everyone and everything into account."

What Poor Decision Making Looks Like

Licia N.
Decision-making score = 1.3

What people who work with her say:

"Licia is rarely able to make a balanced decision. She is either 100% black or 100% white, with no middle ground. She will improve her performance if she can temper her urgency with a more considered approach, taking into account the views of others."

"Licia has a propensity to make definitive decisions based on little or no valid information. Once she makes a decision, it takes a huge effort to get her to change her mind, even after providing her with the actual facts."

"Licia needs to slow down, consider all aspects of a problem equally, and communicate a comprehensive message to all parties involved when implementing new procedures or solving issues. Snap decisions without really understanding how each element affects different departments only undermines efficiency and attitude, and creates future problems that have to be patched or worked around."

Burke F.
Decision-making score = 2

What people who work with him say:
"Burke should gather more input from others when making decisions. He has a tendency to make decisions that affect a significant number of people without thinking through the whole process."

"Many here get the feeling Burke waits too long to make decisions. His decisions are often made at the last minute without enough time to think them through. He proceeds without the facts and bases his decisions on hearsay. He doesn't do his research. If he analyzed his decisions in more depth, the outcome would probably be better."

"Burke has to improve his ability to make fast, accurate decisions. Agility is very important. People who have control of ten-million-dollar businesses have to be able to make quick decisions on buying simple, few-thousand-dollar equipment."

Communication

Communication is the real work of leadership. Communicating is a fundamental element of how leaders

> **You simply can't become a great leader until you are a great communicator.**

accomplish their goals every day. You simply can't become a great leader until you are a great communicator.

Great communicators inspire people. They create a connection with their followers that is real, emotional, and personal regardless of any physical distance between them. Great communicators forge this connection through an understanding of people and an ability to speak directly to their needs in a manner that they are ready to hear.

Good communication skills equip leaders to motivate people to take action on behalf of the organization. The eight strategies that follow will teach you some of the communication secrets of great leaders. Apply these strategies and watch your communication skills reach new heights.

1. Speak to Groups as Individuals

As a leader, you often have to speak to groups of people. Whether a small team meeting or a company-wide gathering, you need to develop a level of intimacy in your approach that makes each individual in the room feel as if you're speaking directly to him or her. The trick is to eliminate the distraction of the crowd so that you can deliver your message just as you would if you were talking to a single person. You want to be emotionally genuine and exude the same feelings, energy, and attention you would one-on-one (as opposed to the anxiety that comes with being in front of people). The ability to pull this off is the hallmark of great leadership communication.

2. Talk so People Will Listen

Great communicators read their audience (groups and individuals) carefully to ensure they aren't wasting their breath on a message that people aren't ready to hear. Talking so people will listen means you adjust your message on the fly to stay with your audience (what they're ready to hear and how they're ready to hear it). Droning on to ensure you've said what you wanted to say does not have the same effect on people as engaging them in a meaningful dialogue in which there is an exchange of ideas. Resist the urge to drive your point home at all costs. When your talking leads to people asking good questions, you know you're on the right track.

3. Listen so People Will Talk

One of the most disastrous temptations for a leader is to treat communication as a one-way street. When you communicate, you must give people ample opportunity to speak their minds. If you find that you're often having the last word in conversations, then this is likely something you need to work on.

Listening isn't just about hearing words; it's also about listening to the tone, speed, and volume of the voice. What is being said? Anything not being said? What hidden messages below the surface exist? When someone is talking to you, stop everything else and listen fully until the other person has finished speaking. When you are on a phone call, don't type an email. When you're meeting with someone, close the door and sit near the person, so you can focus and listen. Simple behaviors like these will help you stay in the present moment, pick up on the cues the other person sends, and make it clear that you will really hear what he or she is saying.

4. Connect Emotionally

Maya Angelou said it best: "People will forget what you said and did, but they will never forget how you made them feel." As a leader, your communication is impotent if people don't connect with it on an emotional level. This is hard for many leaders to pull off because they feel they need to project a certain persona. Let that go. To connect with your people emotionally, you need to be transparent. Be human. Show them what drives you, what you care about, what makes you get out of bed in the morning. Express these feelings openly, and you'll forge an emotional connection with your people.

> **People will forget what you said and did, but they will never forget how you made them feel.**

5. Read Body Language

Your authority makes it hard for people to say what's really on their minds. No matter how good a relationship you have with your subordinates, you are kidding yourself if you think they are as open with you as they are with their peers. So, you must become adept at understanding unspoken messages. The greatest wealth of information lies in people's body language. The body communicates nonstop and is an abundant source of information, so purposefully watch body language during meetings and casual conversation. Once you tune into body language, the messages will become loud and clear. Pay as much attention to what isn't said as what is said, and you'll uncover facts and opinions that people are unwilling to express directly.

6. Prepare Your Intent

A little preparation goes a long way toward saying what you wanted to say and having a conversation achieve its intended impact. Don't prepare a speech; develop an understanding of what the focus of a conversation needs to be and how you will accomplish this. Your communication will be more persuasive and on point when you prepare your intent ahead of time.

7. Skip the Jargon

The business world is filled with jargon and metaphors that are harmless when people can relate to them. Problem is, most leaders overuse jargon and alienate their

> **...most leaders overuse jargon and alienate their subordinates and customers with their "business speak."**

subordinates and customers with their "business speak." Use it sparingly if you want to connect with your people. Otherwise, you'll come across as insincere.

8. Practice Active Listening

Active listening is a simple technique that ensures people feel heard, an essential component of good communication. To practice active listening:

- Spend more time listening than you do talking.

- Do not answer questions with questions.

- Avoid finishing other people's sentences.

- Focus more on the other person than you do on yourself.

- Focus on what people are saying right now, not on what their interests are.

- Reframe what the other person has said to make sure you understand him or her correctly ("So you're telling me that this budget needs further consideration, right?").

- Think about what you're going to say after someone has finished speaking, not while he or she is speaking.

- Ask plenty of questions.

- Never interrupt.

- Don't take notes.

As you work to employ these strategies, try to avoid biting off more than you can chew. Working on one to three strategies at a time is sufficient. If you try to take on more than you can handle, you're not going to see as much progress as you would if you narrowed your focus. Once you become effective in one particular strategy, you can take on another one in its place. Communication is a dynamic element of leadership that is intertwined in most of what you do each day. You'll have ample opportunity to improve your abilities in this critical skill.

What Communication Looks Like

Samantha O.
Communication score = 6*

What people who work with her say:
"Samantha can defuse tense situations and instill confidence in others by the way she communicates and presents herself. She has the ability to adapt her communication style to a variety of personalities to gain consensus and build trust. She follows up on her commitments and touches base with her staff regularly to ask how they're doing and how she can help."

"Samantha is a skilled communicator and is particularly good 'on the hoof' and across multiple cultures. She reads people and situations very well by being a respectful, patient listener. She tells you what she knows and doesn't know."

"After virtually every conversation I have with her, I feel heard, supported, and better about whatever topic we had discussed. She has a knack for reading people and situations to deduce the best approach to take in moving forward. She is clear about things she needs done and is always available to answer questions."

---

* Scores are on the 1- to 6-point scale (1=never and 6=always) from the 360° Refined™ test. Scores represent the average rating received from all who rated the executive. Scores and coworker comments are from actual people, though names and other identifying information have been altered.

Antonio V.
Communication score = 5.7

What people who work with him say:
"I would offer that Antonio is a world-class communicator. He is one of the most effective, infectious, and dynamic speakers I have ever heard. He is effective with large audiences as well as with smaller groups and individual communication. In working with Antonio for several years, we were responsible for presenting various investment products to a wide range of institutional investors. He was always able to connect with his audience no matter who they may have been. He has transferred that skill to presenting our overall corporate message to investors and employees alike."

"Antonio is able to explain complex ideas succinctly to the most senior levels of the organization. He also demonstrates this well in his interactions with outside companies, balancing the line between seeking information, sharing information, and driving his agenda expertly."

"Antonio knows his audience and translates his thoughts into forms the audience can understand. In one email or one short conversation, he is able to achieve multiple goals at the same time: fulfilling responsibility, advocating a position, and making himself available for future discourse."

What a Lack of Communication Looks Like

Nadine N.
Communication score = 1.3

What people who work with her say:

"I often feel as though Nadine is not listening to me or my colleagues. She hears the first word or two of our comments, and then leaps to a conclusion about what we are trying to say that is often off the mark. As a result, it is difficult to make a subtle point to her without having her interrupt you or answer a minor part of your comment that is tangential. She needs to focus on listening carefully and sincerely, as doing so will enable her to communicate much better."

"Nadine needs to communicate and be more responsive to emails, calls, instant messages, etc. She is the hardest person on the planet to track down, plus she is a funnel, as everything needs to go through her. She needs to designate her staff to help her communicate."

"Nadine needs to be more measured in her communication. She has a tendency to dominate discussions during meetings, most often to the detriment of the discussion. I've observed multiple instances when her communication tendencies have derailed meetings and frustrated her peers and the top execs above her."

"Everything is always a spin job with Nadine. You need to know exactly the right question to ask if you expect an answer. She is also extremely slow at response and follow-up, if she even bothers to follow up at all."

Omar D.
Communication score = 1.3

What people who work with him say:
"Omar's thoughts are scattered and lack focus. He usually does not have a solid agenda at meetings, and when he does, he does not stick to it, resulting in a meeting that could be effectively completed in thirty minutes taking at least twice as long. He is confusing at times, and keeps people from asking questions—important questions!"

"Omar's communication style, verbal and written, needs to be more concise and focused. A few times his managers have come to me asking for help understanding his communications. He is not sensitive to his audience, and he seems to drop names and acronyms that his audience either are not familiar with or do not find relevant."

"When a business slowdown and reduction in the workforce were taking place, people were saying that we were going to be laid off. They stated that Omar said it, but no one was willing to ask for verification from Omar. He does not communicate for understanding. He constantly is preaching the 'Five Whys,' but when confronted with an issue, his first word is, 'Who?'"

Mobilizing Others

You can have a well-articulated, even profound, vision for your organization that people can see and understand, but they won't help you achieve it if they aren't engaged. Your ability to mobilize others hinges upon your ability to engage them in their work.

Employee engagement is not to be confused with employee satisfaction. High marks on the company's employee satisfaction survey does not mean your workforce is engaged—these surveys set the bar too low. Satisfied employees will show up and do their jobs without complaint, but that doesn't mean they'll spontaneously give you 110% or turn down another job that offers them a 10% higher salary. People need to feel respected, valued, and emotionally engaged in their work if you want them to mobilize. This requires an emotional commitment to you, their leader, and you can build this commitment with the right tools.

> **High marks on the company's employee satisfaction survey does not mean your workforce is engaged—these surveys set the bar too low.**

When you engage your employees, their discretionary effort kicks in. Discretionary effort supercharges your workforce; it yields pro-organizational behavior that has a profound impact on the bottom line. Research by Towers Perrin found that companies whose workers are engaged have 6% higher profit margins. Doesn't sound like much until you consider that engaging your people doesn't cost a dime. As Doug Conant, the former CEO of Campbell's Soup, said, "To win in the marketplace, you must first win in the workplace."

Employ the following strategies to engage your employees and watch them mobilize as their discretionary effort grows:

1. Give Thanks

Most people say that they rarely, if ever, get thanked for their contributions at work. Yet people also agree that hearing something as simple as "thank you" has a positive impact on their morale. Sometimes the little things really do go a long way, especially when it comes to letting people know they are appreciated. There are people who do great work around you every day. Let them know how you feel about it. Don't hesitate or put it off until next week. Do something this week or even today. Things as simple as a pat on the back or a carefully worded message that sums

> **Most people say that they rarely, if ever, get thanked for their contributions at work.**

up how you feel will help you build fierce loyalty in your people. Recognition elevates the person who receives it; it impacts the recipient as well as all who witness the praise.

2. Be Thoughtful

Being thoughtful is a powerful way to let employees know they are valuable to you. Anything that's important to you is going to be on your mind, and your employees will consider you thoughtful if you let them know that they are on your mind. Here's how you do it:

- Communicate regularly. Meetings, speeches, informal chats, emails, phone calls, tweets, and status updates—they all work.

- Celebrate accomplishments and note progress.

- Share your plans and get people involved in them.

- Share your knowledge and teach people something new.

- Express your appreciation and gratitude.

- Be a reassuring and calming force that people can rely on.

- Be confident and enthusiastic about the future.

- Don't condescend or criticize.

- Do these things every single day and teach others to do the same.

3. Declare Decision Rights

When it comes to responsibilities, clarity breeds confidence, and confusion breeds disillusion. Make certain that everyone knows exactly which decisions and tasks he or she is responsible for. You can't expect people to engage and mobilize when expectations are not abundantly clear. Anytime there is confusion, you should have a process in place for important information to flow back to you so that you can correct the course and get everyone on the same page.

> When it comes to responsibilities, clarity breeds confidence, and confusion breeds disillusion.

4. Earn Their Respect

There is no greater catalyst to commitment and engagement than earning your people's respect. If your people don't respect you (not your status but who you are and how you are as a person), how can you expect them to pursue your vision wholeheartedly? Walk your talk, be respectful, and earn the respect that will make your people want to follow you to the ends of the Earth.

> Walk your talk, be respectful, and earn the respect that will make your people want to follow you to the ends of the Earth.

5. Integrate Ideas

In a knowledge-driven economy, you get work done by synthesizing a diverse set of ideas and interests. Your ability to bring people together and facilitate the integration of their skill sets is critical to your ability to mobilize others. Bring people together as much as you can and solicit their input on the toughest issues the organization is facing. This joint problem solving will make your people feel respected and valued, and their valuable input will be an important benefit to your work.

6. Have an "Open-door" Policy

The Open Door policy originated in 1899 when the United States feared it would lose its trading privileges in East Asia. So, the United States declared an "open-door policy," allowing all trading nations access to the Chinese market. Today, a true open-door policy allows any employee to talk to anyone at any level, fostering upward communication through direct and easy access. When you increase your accessibility through an open-door policy (even when executed virtually), people feel valued and respected because of the time you've given them, and you remain connected to the flow of ideas bubbling up from within the organization.

7. Teach Your Managers to Engage

Your managers can be vessels of employee engagement by showing genuine interest and concern for those who report to them. Whether providing recognition, showing real concern for decisions that have been made, or demonstrating an understanding of the difficulties people are up against, your engagement efforts will fall flat if your managers aren't part of the plan.

8. Only Get Mad on Purpose

"Anyone can become angry—that is easy. But to be angry with the right person, to the right degree, at the right time, for the right purpose, and in the right way, this is not easy." —Aristotle

Anger exists for a reason. If you manage your anger properly and use it purposefully, you can enhance your relationships. Seriously. Think of the football coach who gets straight to the point at halftime. His stern feedback grabs his players' attention and focuses them for the second half. The team returns refreshed, refocused, and

> "Anyone can become angry—that is easy. But to be angry with the right person, to the right degree, at the right time, for the right purpose, and in the right way, this is not easy."—Aristotle

ready to win; in this case, the coach manages his emotions to motivate others to action.

Expressing your anger in appropriate ways effectively illustrates the gravity of a situation. Expressing your anger too much or at the wrong times desensitizes people to your feelings, making it hard for them to take you seriously.

Remember, mobilizing others requires creating a sincere, deep connection with your people. To do this, you need to be honest with yourself and honest with your people, which sometimes requires expressing strong feelings.

Mobilizing others is a skill that builds momentum with time. Start working to engage and mobilize your employees now, and you'll reap the benefits from your efforts for some time to come.

What Mobilizing Others Looks Like

Brenda L.
Mobilizing others score = 6*

What people who work with her say:

"Brenda is great at putting big ideas into action. She is a motivator. She achieves difficult goals not just by herself but also by building a community and encouraging others to join in with their strengths. She is also unusually gifted at knowing what motivates a person to behave a certain way. Brenda is good at recognizing the skills and personality traits of the management team to most effectively position, organize, and motivate them to meet company goals."

"She has this keen ability to make you want to do more and push yourself harder. She listens to what you are saying. She offers to work with you to accomplish a goal. You do not feel like you are out there on your own. She will listen and offer advice or solutions to an issue or problem. While many leaders focus on 'What have you done for me lately?,' Brenda focuses on 'What can I do to help you succeed?' This approach makes a huge difference in motivating me to do my best every single day."

---

* Scores are on the 1- to 6-point scale (1=never and 6=always) from the 360° Refined™ test. Scores represent the average rating received from all who rated the executive. Scores and coworker comments are from actual people, though names and other identifying information have been altered.

"Brenda is a natural motivator. She has a talent for making people feel like there is no task that they are not competent enough to complete, and I think that creates the motivation and desire to do a great job. Her bright attitude and sunny disposition can change the mood of any room and lends itself to inspiring us to get going."

Seth J.
Mobilizing others score = 5.7

What people who work with him say:
"Seth inspires teamwork and is one of those rare leaders who can ask you to put in the extra hour or go the extra mile without you realizing you were asked to give or sacrifice. Many leaders can push a team to a goal, but Seth has the ability to do it in a way that creates an environment of teamwork rather than drudgery. That simple intangible makes all the difference when you realize it is 7 p.m. and the next bus home isn't for an hour."

"Seth is great at motivating me. He really has been a source of encouragement over the past two years. Auditing is at times difficult and at many times a thankless job, but somehow Seth always makes me feel appreciated and that I am making a difference to our company. That makes me want to work even harder knowing that what I do is appreciated."

"It is very easy for him to get a group of people enthused about a project and to keep them motivated to do their best. He is able to do this so well because of the passion he has for what he does. If he is working on something, he gives it his all and that inspires people working with him to want to give 110%."

What a Lack of Mobilizing Others Looks Like

Joyce M.
Mobilizing others score = 1.3

What people who work with her say:

"Joyce does not generate followers. She doesn't inspire her teams to learn and become involved. She needs to learn all aspects of the businesses. She needs to know what makes people tick and have her finger on the pulse of what main issues reside in each business unit (and what works well) so that she can truly understand how to move her staff to support them."

"She doesn't inspire me to do my best work. I don't feel she cares about me personally or professionally. She doesn't foster an environment of risk taking or collaboration on our team."

"Joyce has to learn what motivates others. It is not all about her goals all the time. Closing facilities is sometimes the easy thing to do but not always the right thing to do for the long-term success of the company."

Keith R.
Mobilizing others score = 2

What people who work with him say:

"We are people, too, and most of the time Keith doesn't see that. It all seems like personal gain for him. No one likes the way he talks down to us, or at least I don't. I hear no words of encouragement. If there is a problem, we hear it, or I should say we overhear him telling someone else, but when we do something good, there is never a 'great job.'"

"Keith just hasn't mastered getting people behind him. He doesn't understand what each of his people need as far as recognition and motivation to get the most out of everyone."

"He doesn't set a great example of how much he expects from us—because he doesn't do much himself. I think this is why Keith can't get people behind new policies."

4
Results

Sometimes you build a complete and compelling vision, you create a sound strategy, and you mobilize your people to pursue important objectives, yet results fail to materialize. Most leaders left in this predicament (scratching their heads, we might add) chalk the lack of results up to market forces beyond their control. What these leaders don't realize is that the invisible barrier that stands between them and results is something they've created through their own actions.

With the correct building blocks in place, results will materialize only if you possess the finesse that comes from three essential skills. The first is the ability to take risks, especially *the right risks*. The second is the ability to maintain what we call a "results focus," or how adept you are at keeping everyone's eyes on the prize. The final skill is agility, which anyone can attest is an essential leadership skill now.

Risk Taking

Most leaders have a hard time understanding why they are deficient in the skill of risk taking because they don't see themselves as risk averse. It's true—the average leader is more risk prone than risk averse; leaders just don't take risks in all the areas they should. Risk taking as a skill is about taking the right risks, and this requires learning to see yourself and your work in new ways.

Leaders must learn to take all kinds of risks, not just those that involve business strategies. To be a well-rounded leader, you need to be a well-rounded risk taker. Take risks in how you interact with people—be more vulnerable, open to feedback, and connected with your employees. This will require you to move out of your comfort zone and experience new things. The strategies that follow will help you up your risk-taking game in all of the areas essential to your effectiveness as a leader. Many require taking the blinders off and tolerating the discomfort that comes with learning a new approach to your job and your people—that is risk taking in its highest form.

> **Leaders must learn to take all kinds of risks, not just those that involve business strategies.**

1. Replace Ego with Authenticity

To get the results you desire, take a huge personal risk, and drop the ego. Your ego is a defense that shelters you from the world around you. That façade operates like a set of blinders and allows you to see

> **Pride and arrogance are replaced by authenticity and transparency, two qualities that get results every time.**

only where you point your head. With the bulk of your vision obscured, you miss major opportunities—all because you're afraid to see something that you won't like. When you lose the ego, you see the whole picture. Pride and arrogance are replaced by authenticity and transparency, two qualities that get results every time.

2. Face Your Fear of Failure

Fear of failure is the primary reason successful people stall out in their careers. This paralyzing emotion enables opportunities to evaporate right before their eyes. It's ironic that, in spite of their track record, so many successful people fall victim to this fear. Living in your comfort zone is a massive barrier between you and the ability to reach your goals. Facing your fear of failure is a powerful way to take a huge leap right out of your comfort zone.

3. Take a Leap

If you have trouble taking risks, you need to learn to tolerate uncertainty. Everyone has a comfort zone that provides him or her with a sense of safety and security. You can't grow as a leader until you move out of this comfort zone. You can never be 100% certain about the best course of action for any decision you make. Even when you feel 100% certain of something, this feeling isn't based on data—it's merely a representation of your confidence. When you're risk averse, it takes you too long to build the confidence you need to act. In the areas where you're having trouble taking risks, try taking action when you're only 70% certain it's the right way to go. What feels like 70% certainty to you feels like 100% certainty to someone who isn't hesitant to take appropriate risks. When you're risk averse, adopting this 70% strategy is a great way to move forward without waiting too long to act.

4. Take a Small Leap

If you can't tolerate taking a leap and moving forward with 70% certainty, search for smaller risks where you can tolerate this level of uncertainty. The trick is, you can't stay there. You need to work your way up to larger and larger risks until you're able to operate at the speed of your peers.

5. Don't Lose Sight of the Long Term

If you tend to act impulsively and thus make poor decisions, you need to shift your sights to the long term. Often the worst decisions that leaders make are those that achieve

> **Often the worst decisions that leaders make are those that achieve short-term gain at the expense of long-term strategy.**

short-term gain at the expense of long-term strategy. Don't throw away your future for a fleeting moment in the sun.

6. Acknowledge Mistakes

Acknowledging mistakes is a risk leaders are hesitant to take because they fear it won't be well received. It's a risk worth taking. Acknowledging your mistakes quickly and courageously lets people know you're human. This humble action creates a powerful, lasting connection with your people. To build yourself up to take this risk, just remember the words of Pablo Picasso, "I am always doing that which I cannot do, in order that I may learn how to do it."

7. Get Personal

Many leaders have been taught to keep people at arm's length. This ideology is based on fear—fear that people getting to know you will undermine your authority if they don't like what they see. The truth is, the opposite happens. When people get to know all of you (when they see the beauty and the blemishes), they become fiercely loyal to you and your cause. The old axiom is true: "People don't

> **People don't care how much you know until they know how much you care.**

care how much you know until they know how much you care." Getting personal and real with your employees shows them that you respect and value their contributions. You just need to take the risk and stop keeping people at arm's length, stop giving them sanitized versions of the truth, and start having meaningful face-to-face interactions with your employees.

8. Tell Hard Truths

The fear most leaders claim to have about sharing the gravity of the challenges their organization is facing is that doing so will cause employees to jump ship. The truth is most leaders just want to keep things running smoothly for as long as they possibly can, and managing employee reactions to hard truths is not a simple task. Enabling your employees to tackle tough problems head-on is a risk you should take. As long as you're calculated in what you share and how you share it, taking this risk will empower your people and inspire them to take action to improve what they can.

In the end, your ability to take risks effectively is going to hinge on your willingness to live outside your comfort zone. This means taking risks in areas where you're typically risk averse and keeping yourself in check in the areas where you're too risk prone.

What Risk Taking Looks Like

Wayne R.
Risk-taking score = 6*

What people who work with him say:

"Wayne is very brave and can say things we only think about. He is willing to take the risk but with the intention of improving the situation. I really appreciate working with him and watching him in action."

"Wayne is excellent at pushing the envelope to make the business succeed and help people exceed their goals. He has made very good strides in creating opportunities to grow the business during very difficult economic times in the past few years."

"Wayne is great at taking risks while managing them and implementing risk strategies. There are examples I could give related to emergency situations when he isn't afraid to take the risks necessary to resolve the crisis."

Gloria G.
Risk-taking score = 5.9

What people who work with her say:
"Gloria is very confident in where she is going, which helps others feel safe to follow her. She is not afraid to take risks or think of new and innovative ways to make things happen."

"She's great at taking calculated risks and building consensus among the members of the team. This combination helps her get the best possible outcome."

"Gloria has a great ability to step outside the box and push the envelope when it comes to ideas. For instance, with the fund-raiser she and her team dressed up in firefighter outfits to get people's attention. It was a risk that really worked well."

What a Lack of Risk Taking Looks Like

Joanne K.
Risk-taking score = 1.3

What people who work with her say:

"Joanne holds herself back by not being a risk taker. She needs to develop the mindset that sometimes she'll need to take the leap instead of doing only what feels safe."

"Joanne should take the lead more often. She should take the risk of stating her position on an issue, even if it evokes disagreement among the management team."

"I wish Joanne would be more willing to take a risk if she felt that it was values driven. She appears concerned with impressing or saying the right thing to the right people simply to be liked or in good favor with certain people. Joanne needs to have confidence, step up, and take risks. I think she will be surprised at what she can accomplish."

* Scores are on the 1- to 6-point scale (1=never and 6=always) from the 360° Refined™ test. Scores represent the average rating received from all who rated the executive. Scores and coworker comments are from actual people, though names and other identifying information have been altered.

Lewis T.
Risk-taking score = 2

What people who work with him say:
"Lewis seems afraid to make a decision unless all of the information is known, which is never the case. He has been a bit too risk averse over the past couple of months. Not everything is black and white. He needs to get more comfortable with taking risks when decisions lie in the gray."

"I think that if Lewis is being held back it is from taking too little risk. He doesn't move out of his comfort zone. I think that he can do more and produce more from his function's campaigns than he is now."

"I wish Lewis would experiment a little more to push the envelope on some campaigns. We need to test some new and crazy things that could be very successful campaigns."

Results Focus

As a leader, you not only have to keep your eyes on the prize to see important objectives through to fruition, but you also have to ensure the same for your people. This can be a challenge, especially when you factor in the unique motivations and interests that each employee brings. Everyone wants results, but the leaders who build a sense of utter and complete focus in their people are the ones who get it done. The strategies that follow will help you make it happen.

> **Everyone wants results, but the leaders who build a sense of utter and complete focus in their people are the ones who get it done.**

1. Frame Your Ideas

Framing is the process of guiding what someone is likely to think about what you are saying through the careful use of expression. Framing puts boundaries around what's discernible in your message, much like a picture frame does for a picture. For example, a mayoral candidate might say she's "tough on crime," which has a different connotation from her competitor saying he's going to "create safe neighborhoods." They're likely going to do the same thing, but you'll think about each candidate differently based upon how his or her message is framed.

If you teach your people "the customer is king," that will guide them in a different direction from telling them to "treat the customer like you would your own mother." The intended meaning is the same with each frame, but the results are going to be altogether different because the choice of words guides people's thinking in different directions. In your quest to keep people focused on results, use language that frames your message with the correct connotation. Otherwise, you may find your people are headed in a different direction than you intended.

2. Maintain a Presence

Never underestimate the value of face time. Woody Allen quipped that 80% of success is just showing up, and this is true for leaders who want to keep their people's focus aligned. Your busy schedule ensures your people do not receive the amount of face time that they need. Whether you're across town, across the globe, or in the conference room on the next floor, your accessibility is limited. When you're out of town, you need to have a policy that people can reach out to you freely, and you

> **Never underestimate the value of face time.**

need to back it up by being accessible (and not annoyed by the inevitable interruptions). When you're in the office, you need to be present, giving people your full attention, interest, and enthusiasm. Make certain you leave your office and go see your team. Face-to-face communication is a powerful way to get your point across and make certain that it sticks. Face time enables you to take the pulse of your organization and show leadership. If you can't maintain a presence, you'll wonder why your people's focus wanes.

3. Communicate Early and Often

Like it or not, your people need to hear from you often, and this can be difficult to accommodate when your schedule pulls you in 18 different directions. When you don't communicate adequately (or are slow to respond to requests for information), you allow someone else to frame the situation for you. Chances are, he or she isn't going to provide the answers you would have, and this has an impact upon your ability to get results. So, make a point of reaching out to people, and make yourself accessible so that people will reach out to you regardless of where your job takes you.

4. Speak in the Affirmative

When your message fixates on obstacles, challenges, and barriers, you give these things power over your people. People want to hear what's possible—they aspire to achieve. So don't let them get bogged down by what's standing in their way. Speak in the affirmative by focusing on what you will accomplish and what you will do to accomplish it. This gives power to the positive actions you want people to take and emboldens them to take action.

> When your message fixates on obstacles, challenges, and barriers, you give these things power over your people.

5. Praise Results-focused Behavior

One manager comes to you shortly before a project deadline to request an extension. Another comes up with a creative way to reanalyze the data and produce the report on time. Employees who are results focused aim all of their attention at the result they wish to achieve and won't allow anything to stand in their way. Praise those who demonstrate this skill and watch it catch on.

6. Be Specific

For leaders, vagueness is a vice. Train yourself to use clarity when speaking to your team. Even the simplest actions can become muddled when your directives lack clarity. It's one thing to say, "Let's work to improve our communication," and another entirely to say, "To improve our communication, let's gather on Tuesdays and Thursdays at 2 p.m. to check in with each other." If you want to get results, you need to be abundantly clear when stating what you wish to accomplish.

7. Give Quality Feedback

Leaders often sell themselves short by assuming that providing feedback is a managerial task. If you are truly focused on results, then you'll want to take every opportunity you can to help people understand how they are supporting the total picture. Be clear with your feedback. Don't soften it to avoid confrontation. Be quick to stroke people who are on the right track. You are a leader. It's your job to ensure your people are on the road to results. Just remember, feedback is meant to address the problem, not the person. Keep your message clear, direct, constructive, and respectful.

8. Follow Through

There are many reasons to follow through and do what you say you are going to do, but it's impossible to overstate the importance of follow-through for a leader who wants his or her people focused on results. Follow-through is about creating accountability. When you don't follow through, you make it clear to your people that "there's no accountability here." Leaders who don't walk

> **Leaders who don't walk their talk breed cynicism and resentment—two negative emotional states that will squash people's desire to pursue your important objectives.**

their talk breed cynicism and resentment—two negative emotional states that will squash people's desire to pursue your important objectives.

What Results Focus Looks Like

Miguel F.
Results-focus score = 5.8*

What people who work with him say:

"Miguel is very driven to attain results and instills a similar drive in his team. We can always count on him to push beyond a goal and seek the best results possible. I think Miguel is an asset to the leadership team, in part because of the way he attains goals. Part of this is his unwillingness to accept 'no'—he is willing to push the envelope to get the desired result. This skill is essential to our company's success."

"Miguel is great at bulldogging a problem and making sure that the end result is achieved. He is relentless in seeking to meet deadlines and fulfill obligations. This is not limited to any single example, because it is the way Miguel operates day in and day out. He led an understaffed team to outperform regions that were fully staffed."

"This product launch was the biggest effort in the industry in the last several years. Without Miguel running it, it would have likely languished and gone on for several years

* Scores are on the 1- to 6-point scale (1=never and 6=always) from the 360° Refined™ test. Scores represent the average rating received from all who rated the executive. Scores and coworker comments are from actual people, though names and other identifying information have been altered.

like its predecessor. He stayed on top of the entire broad effort, resolved issues, removed obstacles, and held the managers and vendors accountable for delivering on their commitments."

"When Miguel's managing a product launch, he stays on top of things, regularly gathers status updates, has checkpoints, manages dependencies, and resolves any problems that come up. He is passionate about excellence and looks for solutions that preserve the business goal. He's obsessive about delivering on his commitments. He executes and finishes."

Lorena R.
Results-focus score = 5.5

What people who work with her say:
"Lorena is amazing at driving and obtaining results. She is awesome in her role. Even under massive pressure or with many obstacles in the way, she will carry forward to try and achieve a goal that she believes in. In addition, she figures out who she needs to engage with in order to achieve that goal."

"Lorena is results oriented and focused on delivering—and she measures herself that way, which is a huge strength. Lorena can hold people accountable to operational tasks and get results. She says what's on her mind and is clear about the direction. She backs you 100% as long as you have done your homework. She also gets results from other departments on key operational issues."

"Lorena is focused on what is important in order to get results and challenges staff to operate with a long-term perspective. She works collaboratively across the business unit structure to create the conditions for the team to be effective."

What a Lack of Results Focus Looks Like

Amy C.
Results-focus score = 2.3

What people who work with her say:

"She tries to be seen as people-oriented and neglects being task oriented to achieve department and company results. For example, she does not give instructions on how to carry out activities and ends with no outcomes at the end of meetings. In manufacturing areas, she has to be task-oriented to bring the area to the next level of performance."

"Amy is a good conceptual thinker, but translating this to action is a problem. She needs to be more focused on achieving results. She needs to have a plan and work the plan—her approach is unstructured."

"Amy is not able to drive results through others. We have had a significant underperforming manufacturing organization that she needs to lead to a better result. She really thinks she is the best, no improvement needed."

Bogdan L.
Results-focus score = 1.5

What people who work with him say:
"Bogdan is too passive to be a leader, and does not consistently take control of a situation to deliver results. He should develop skills to influence others to perform. Currently, he is very task oriented but can easily lose sight of the bigger initiative and its critical path. He should focus primarily on keeping his finger on the pulse of the effort, and ensuring results are delivered, rather than getting too deep into technical tasks."

"Bogdan seems to have a low energy level. He is reluctant to roll up his sleeves to take massive action to achieve results."

"Bogdan regularly comes to work late, which doesn't set a good example for his team and gives the idea that he may not be fully engaged. He should push for better results rather than delivering what's expected. If something can be better, he should go for it more often. He'd get better results if he challenged his people to optimize results."

Agility

As a leader, you must be agile to do your job effectively. Without agility, you won't excel, and in fast-moving markets, you are unlikely to survive. Leaders are called on to show others the way, and you can't do this if you dig your heels in every time something unexpected happens.

None of us is born with a crystal ball that predicts the future. Since you can't foresee every change and every obstacle that life throws your way, the key to remaining flexible and navigating change successfully is your perspective *before* changes surface.

> **Leaders are called on to show others the way, and you can't do this if you dig your heels in every time something unexpected happens.**

The first step is to admit to yourself that even the most stable, trusted facets of your work life are not completely under your control. People change, business ebbs and flows, and things just don't stay the same for long. When you equip yourself to anticipate change (and understand your options when changes occur), you prevent yourself from getting bogged down by emotions like shock, surprise, fear, and resentment when changes actually happen. Although you're still likely to experience these negative emotions, your acceptance that change is an inevitable part of life enables you to focus and think rationally, which is critical to making the most out of an unlikely, unwanted, or otherwise unforeseen situation. As a leader, you set the emotional tone for your people, and if you go running around like the sky is falling every time things change, your people will do the same.

However, agility isn't just about being flexible in response to changes in your external environment. Agility is also about the changes that can happen in you. One of the biggest keys to your success is your ability to grow and adapt with your position. This requires a level of personal flexibility that most people do not have to develop during their careers.

The strategies that follow will help you develop the agility you need as a leader.

1. Make Change Your Muse

Since change is inevitable, why not seek it out? Being the first to spot a trend means you can also be the first to capitalize on it, but you have to be on the lookout for this to happen. If you wait for change to land in your lap, it's too late. The idea here is to prepare for change. Make change your inspiration. It's empowering to react swiftly and effectively to change. It's also a great way to snatch competitive advantage.

2. Think through Consequences

When you think through the consequences of potential changes, you can act decisively when the changes surface. Set aside a small amount of time regularly to create a list of important changes that could possibly happen. Leave enough room below each change on your list to write out all the possible actions you will take should the change occur. Then below that, jot down ideas for things that you can do now to prepare for that change. Consider the signs you can keep an eye out for that suggest these changes are imminent. These warning signs will cue you in as the likelihood of the change increases. Even if the changes on your list never come to fruition, just anticipating change and knowing what you'll do in response to it makes you a more flexible and adaptive leader.

3. Address Uncertainty Head-on

The bend at the end of the road is not the end of the road unless you refuse to take the turn. When things change, or are about to change, your people need to know about it. Don't be afraid to discuss these unexpected course corrections just because you can't keep them from happening.

Change is a critical time for you to be visible, sharing openly and honestly with your people. You and your people should troubleshoot the situation together. Doing so shows respect and consideration for your employees, and their input opens up new perspectives that you might not have otherwise considered. You should create the expectation that uncertainty and change are normal parts of business life and you expect your people to respond flexibly and proactively to them. The alternative—trying to protect your people from change—has the unintended consequences of creating a culture of secrecy and rigidity.

4. Separate Emotion from Reason

The more unexpected and significant a change you're facing, the more likely you are to experience your emotions swaying you in one direction while your rational mind pulls you in another. In these instances, you need to get yourself grounded to ensure your decision making is sound. A good way to do this is to make a list that distinguishes the emotional side of the argument from the rational one. The list will allow you to clear your mind, use your knowledge, and take into account the importance of your emotions without letting them take control.

5. Seek Guidance from the Agile

You'd go to a colleague for industry knowledge or strategic insight, so why not get some guidance from someone who's adept at dealing with change? One of the most powerful ways to learn agility is to seek out the agile and learn their tricks. People who are flexible in dealing with change are usually very aware of what they do, which makes it easy for you to learn from them. Find a person whom you've seen demonstrate great agility and offer to take him or her out for lunch or coffee. During the meeting, share your specific goals for improved agility and ask what tactics he or she relies on. Be certain to be candid about the situations that give you the most trouble.

> **You'd go to a colleague for industry knowledge or strategic insight, so why not get some guidance from someone who's adept at dealing with change?**

6. Adapt Your Leadership Style to the Situation

The best leaders are adept at tailoring their leadership styles to the unique needs of their employees. Unfortunately, this is not the norm. Research conducted by the Ken Blanchard Companies shows that half of leaders are completely inflexible in their approach to leadership and just 25% of leaders have a great deal of variety in their leadership approach. As a leader, you need to have the agility to adjust your style to the needs of the person and the situation. Without a flexible approach to leadership, you greatly limit your ability to get the most from your people.

7. Seek to Maximize Potential

So many times, you can't change a situation or even the parties involved, but that doesn't mean it's time for you to give up. When you find yourself thinking that you have no control, take a closer look at how you are reacting to the situation itself. Focusing on restrictions is not only demoralizing—it also helps negative feelings surface that confirm your sense of helplessness. You must take accountability for what you have control over and focus your energy on remaining flexible and open-minded in spite of the situation. This enables you to maximize the potential that lies before you. Things may have just gotten worse, but that doesn't mean you can't change them for the better.

> **You must take accountability for what you have control over and focus your energy on remaining flexible and open-minded in spite of the situation.**

8. Speak to Someone Who Is Not Affected by the Change

When things change suddenly, your brain is constantly thinking, constantly sorting and analyzing information to decide the best course of action. The problem is, the only information your brain has to go on is what you've given it—what you've seen before and what's happening now. The way our minds are structured, it's far too easy to get stuck on a single train of thought. Allow this to happen, and you're severely limiting your options. It's no wonder that it can be such a relief to talk to someone who is not directly affected by your situation. Not only is it helpful to talk to someone who cares about what you are feeling, but new perspectives also open up additional avenues for you to explore.

When change happens, seek out someone whom you trust and feel comfortable with who is not personally affected by your situation. Use this person as a sounding board for what you've experienced, how you're feeling about the change, and what you're thinking of doing in response to it. Choose your third party wisely. The person you invite to help you shouldn't have a vested interest in the situation; otherwise, his or her perspective is going to be tainted by his or her own needs and feelings. You should also avoid someone you know will simply agree with you. Although the support feels good, it keeps you from seeing the whole picture. Sitting down with a potential devil's advocate may irk you in the moment, but you'll fare far better having seen things from a unique perspective.

What Agility Looks Like

Silas R.
Agility score = 5.9*

What people who work with him say:

"Silas is able to adapt as changes occur and he grasps what's important at an early stage, which allows him to be very effective. His strong points include fostering performance while managing change."

"Silas has been very supportive in a difficult year of change. His adaptability and willingness to go along with a great deal of turmoil and sometimes confusion are greatly appreciated by everyone who works for him. He has a great positive outlook."

"Silas adapts quickly and is willing to change for new requirements called for by a company goal. He understands technology and can communicate what to expect from the changes to the rest of the organization."

* Scores are on the 1- to 6-point scale (1=never and 6=always) from the 360° Refined™ test. Scores represent the average rating received from all who rated the executive. Scores and coworker comments are from actual people, though names and other identifying information have been altered.

Petra A.
Agility score = 5.7

What people who work with her say:
"Petra has a natural talent for seeing an opportunity in every situation, even if the opportunity is not immediate. She adapts to the situation at hand and adjusts her approach to suit the people at each meeting. If a client is reserved and quiet, Petra is great at extracting information without being pushy. If a client is more extroverted, Petra is great at stepping back to let the client do most of the talking."

"Thanks to Petra, the company has been able to remain agile and embrace the future. Without Petra, I don't feel like the company would have been dynamic enough to survive over the years."

"Petra is great at many things. Most importantly, the ability to adapt to a fluid working environment and changing business priorities. I've also been thoroughly impressed with her ability to maintain a positive attitude and provide inspiration. I have very high confidence in her abilities."

What a Lack of Agility Looks Like

Elyse J.
Agility score = 2.3

What people who work with her say:
"Elyse tries to find structure and a rigid path where none exist. Flexibility in this environment is critical to business success. Adaptation to change is difficult to achieve when documentation of a policy is her primary goal."

"Elyse should adapt better to the ways others work, including how she interacts with clients. She usually likes to do things her way, and sometimes lacks the ability to see other people's methods. I would also like to see her figure out how to work as a team when dealing with a client rather than appearing inflexible."

"She doesn't adapt to our always-changing business and doesn't allow herself to expand what she achieves in this new industry."

Chester D.
Agility score = 1.7

What people who work with him say:
"Chester may want to consider being more flexible and working with others who are considering new strategies to help the organization move forward. He is often focused on protecting his own team so much that he loses the forest through the trees."

"Chester needs to not take things so personally, be more flexible, and make adjustments where needed. When our CEO wants him to reprioritize a project, Chester should always respond quickly and readily with adaptability, calling on all and any resources required to achieve the requested results. Instead, he's always trying to do things the way he always has."

"Chester is too rigid. His unwillingness to explore new avenues for the business unnecessarily stresses his and other teams and negatively impacts the entire organization's ability to progress."

ADAPTIVE LEADERSHIP

5
EMOTIONAL INTELLIGENCE

For an adaptive leader, there is no more important skill than emotional intelligence (EQ). Emotional intelligence is your ability to recognize and understand emotions in yourself and others, and your ability to use this awareness to manage your behavior and relationships. Emotional intelligence is the "something" in each of us that is a bit intangible. It affects how we demonstrate self-control, navigate social complexities, and make personal decisions that achieve positive results.

The daily challenge of dealing effectively with emotions is critical to leadership because our brains are hardwired to give emotions the upper hand. Here's how it works: everything you see, smell, hear, taste, and touch travels through your body in the form of electric signals. These signals pass from cell to cell until they reach their ultimate destination, your brain. They enter your brain at the base near your spinal cord, but

> **The daily challenge of dealing effectively with emotions is critical to leadership because our brains are hardwired to give emotions the upper hand.**

must travel across your brain before reaching the place where rational, logical thinking takes place. The trouble is, they pass through your limbic system (the place where emotions are processed) along the way. This journey ensures you experience things emotionally before your reason can kick into gear.

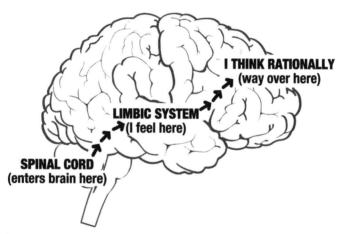

I THINK RATIONALLY
(way over here)

LIMBIC SYSTEM
(I feel here)

SPINAL CORD
(enters brain here)

The physical pathway for emotional intelligence starts in the brain, at the spinal cord. Your primary senses enter here and must travel to the front of your brain before you can think rationally about your experience. However, first they travel through your limbic system, the place where emotions are experienced. Emotional intelligence requires effective communication between the rational and emotional centers of the brain.

The rational area of your brain (the front of your brain) can't stop the emotion "felt" by your limbic system, but the two areas do influence each other and maintain constant communication. The communication between your rational and emotional "brains" is the physical source of emotional intelligence.

Since our brains are wired to make us emotional creatures, your first reaction to an event is always going to be emotional. You have no control over this part of the process. You *do* control the thoughts that follow an emotion, and you have a great deal of say in how you react to an emotion—as long as you are aware of it. Some experiences produce emotions that you are easily aware of; other times, emotions may seem nonexistent. When something generates a strong emotional reaction in you, it's called a "trigger event." Your reaction to your triggers is shaped by your personal history, which includes your experience with similar situations. As your EQ skills grow, you'll learn to spot your triggers and practice productive ways of responding that will become habitual.

Emotional intelligence taps into a fundamental element of human behavior that is distinct from your intellect. There is no known connection between IQ and EQ; you simply can't predict EQ based on how smart someone is. Cognitive intelligence, or IQ, is not flexible. Your IQ, short of a traumatic event such as a brain injury, is fixed from an early age. You don't get smarter by learning new facts or information. Intelligence is your *ability* to learn, and it's the same (relative to your peers) at age 15 as it is at age 50. EQ, on the other hand, is a flexible skill that is readily learned. Although some people are naturally more emotionally intelligent than others, you can develop a high EQ even if you aren't born with it.

When emotional intelligence was first discovered, it served as the missing link in a peculiar finding: people with the highest IQs outperform those with average IQs just 20% of the time, while people with average IQs outperform those with the highest IQs 70% of the time. This anomaly threw a massive wrench into what many people had always assumed was the source of success—IQ. Scientists realized there must be another variable that explained success above and beyond one's IQ, and years of research and numerous studies pointed to EQ as the critical factor.

> **people with the highest IQs outperform those with average IQs just 20% of the time, while people with average IQs outperform those with the highest IQs 70% of the time.**

No matter whether people measure high or low in EQ, they can work to improve it, and those who score low can actually catch up to their coworkers. Researchers at the business school at the University of Queensland in Australia discovered that people who are low in EQ and demonstrate poorer job performance can match their colleagues who excel in both—solely by working to improve their EQ.

Of all the people we've studied at work, we have found that 90% of top performers are also high in EQ. On the flip side, just 20% of bottom performers are high in EQ. You can be a top performer without EQ, but the chances are slim. People who develop their EQ tend to be successful on the job because the two go hand in hand. Naturally, people with high EQ make more money—an average of $29,000 more per year than people with low EQ. The link between EQ and earnings is so direct that every point increase in EQ adds $1,300 on average to an annual salary. These findings hold true for leaders in all industries in every region of the world. We haven't yet been able to find a job in which performance and pay aren't tied closely to EQ. As you might expect, emotional intelligence is more important to success in leadership positions than any other skill.

> **Of all the people we've studied at work, we have found that 90% of top performers are also high in EQ.**

Of the 12 skills that define adaptive leadership, four are emotional intelligence skills. The four emotional intelligence skills pair up under two primary competencies: personal competence and social competence. Personal competence is made up of your self-awareness and self-management skills, which focus more on you individually than on your interactions with other people. Personal competence is your ability to stay aware of your emotions and manage your behavior and tendencies. Social competence is made up of your social awareness and relationship management skills; social competence is your ability to understand other people's moods, behavior, and motives to proactively improve the quality of your relationships.

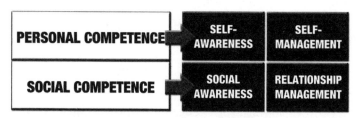

The four skills that make up emotional intelligence. The top two skills, self-awareness and self-management, are more about you. The bottom two skills, social awareness and relationship management, are more about how you are with other people.

Self-awareness

Self-awareness is your ability to accurately perceive your own emotions in the moment and understand your tendencies across situations. Self-awareness includes staying on top of your typical reactions to specific events, challenges, and people. A keen understanding of your tendencies is important; it helps you quickly make sense of your emotions.

Self-awareness is not about discovering deep, dark secrets or unconscious motivations; rather, it comes from developing a straightforward and honest understanding of what makes you tick. Leaders high in self-awareness are remarkably clear in their understanding of what they do well, what motivates and satisfies them, and which people and situations push their buttons.

Self-awareness is a foundational skill: when you have it, self-awareness makes the other emotional intelligence skills much easier to use and the other adaptive leadership skills easier to incorporate into your repertoire. As self-awareness increases, people's satisfaction with life—defined as their ability to reach their goals at work and at home—skyrockets. Self-awareness is so important for job performance that 83% of people high in self-awareness are top performers, and just 2% of bottom performers are high in self-awareness. When you are self-aware, you are far more likely to pursue the right opportunities, put your strengths to work, and—perhaps most importantly—keep your emotions from holding you back.

> **Self-awareness is a foundational skill: when you have it, self-awareness makes the other emotional intelligence skills much easier to use and the other adaptive leadership skills easier to incorporate into your repertoire.**

To be self-aware is to know yourself as you really are. Initially, self-awareness can come across as a somewhat ambiguous concept. There is no finish line where someone is going to slap a medal on you and deem you a "self-aware" leader. In addition, awareness of yourself is not just knowing that you're a people person. It's deeper than that. Getting to know yourself inside and out is a continuous journey of peeling back the layers of the onion and becoming more and more comfortable with what is in the middle—the true essence of you.

Your hardwired emotional reactions to anything come before you even have a chance to respond. Since it isn't possible to leave your emotions out of the equation, managing yourself and your relationships means you first need to be aware of the full range of your feelings, both positive and negative.

The need for self-awareness in leaders has never been greater. Guided by the mistaken notion that psychology deals exclusively with pathology, we assume that the only time to learn about ourselves is in the face of crisis. We tend to embrace those things with which we're comfortable, and put the blinders on the moment something makes us uncomfortable. But it's really

> **The more you understand the beauty and the blemishes, the better you are able to achieve your full potential as a leader.**

the whole picture that serves us. The more you understand the beauty and the blemishes, the better you are able to achieve your full potential as a leader.

The strategies that follow will help you increase your self-awareness and increase the alignment between what you know about yourself and what others see.

1. Lean into Discomfort

A high degree of self-awareness requires a willingness to discover things about yourself that you aren't currently aware of. This can be unsettling at times, especially when you discover things that you'd like to improve. In these moments, just remember that you can't improve your self-awareness without broadening your self-knowledge, and any discomfort you experience means you're moving in the right direction. This effort will be well worth it as increasing your self-awareness will make it much easier to increase your abilities in the other adaptive leadership skills.

2. Listen to What Your Emotions Are Telling You

When you don't take time out to notice and understand your emotions, they have a strange way of resurfacing when you least expect or want them to. It's their way of trying to bring something important to your attention. They will persist, and the damage will mount, until you take notice.

> **When you don't take time out to notice and understand your emotions, they have a strange way of resurfacing when you least expect or want them to.**

When you get a nagging feeling, focus on it until you uncover the source of the feeling (why you are feeling this way). You'll be surprised by how quickly and definitively understanding an emotion strips away its power.

3. Uncover the Source of Your Emotions

Emotions are a great source of data. The only way to genuinely understand your emotions is to spend enough time thinking through them to figure out where they are coming from and why they are there. Emotions always serve a purpose. Many times they seem to arise out of thin air, and it's important to understand why something gets a reaction out of you. Adaptive leaders who do this well can cut to the core of a feeling quickly. Situations that create strong emotions will often require more thought, and these prolonged periods of self-reflection can keep you from doing something that you'll regret.

4. Celebrate Small Victories

Facing the truth about who you are and how you operate can at times be unsettling. Getting in touch with your emotions and tendencies takes honesty and courage. Be patient and give yourself credit for even the smallest amounts of forward momentum. Starting to notice things about yourself that you weren't previously aware of (things you aren't always going to like) means you are progressing. Take pride in this.

5. Uncover Your Primal Leadership

Like it or not, your emotional state as a leader has a contagious effect upon everyone in your organization. Just as people look to leaders for guidance and direction, their emotions are primed by the emotional state of the leaders they follow. Get familiar with all of the ways in which your emotions prime the emotional state of your people.

> Like it or not, your emotional state as a leader has a contagious effect upon everyone in your organization.

6. Go Make Some Mistakes

The surprising thing about self-awareness is that just thinking about it helps you improve the skill, even though much of your focus initially tends to be on what you do "wrong." Having self-awareness means you aren't afraid of your emotional "mistakes." They tell you what you should be doing differently and provide the steady stream of information you need to understand the impact you are having as a leader.

7. Get Feedback

Objective, constructive feedback is a powerful tool for increasing your self-awareness. Such feedback is also a scarce commodity for leaders, because fear of reprisal (real or imagined) keeps people from speaking their minds. Your peers and boss will likely be honest with you if you schedule some time for a chat, explain that you are working on your self-awareness, and ask pointed questions. As for your direct reports, you're better off collecting feedback through an anonymous, constructive tool such as the 360° Refined™ assessment that came with this book. The feedback you receive if you unlock the full assessment will open your eyes to things you would otherwise never have the chance to discover.

8. You Spot It, You Got It

When you're ready for a real self-awareness challenge, pay careful attention to the things that other people do that irk or annoy you. With all the quirky and unusual things that people do every day, you'd think that they'd constantly annoy you. Instead, only select things that people do really get your goat. These things annoy you because they reveal something that you don't like about yourself. The next time people drive you bonkers, think about what it is that they are doing and how this reveals something that you don't like about yourself. Typically, you'll find (if you look hard enough) that you do the same thing they're doing.

> **When you're ready for a real self-awareness challenge, pay careful attention to the things that other people do that irk or annoy you.**

If you truly work to increase your self-awareness, it is a life-altering experience and one that you will not regret. What you learn about yourself will have a profound impact upon your leadership.

What Self-awareness Looks Like

Alton K.
Self-awareness score = 5.5*

What people who work with him say:
"Alton is very aware of his emotional state and how it will affect the team. If he's having a bad day, he warns people. He stays incredibly composed when people around him aren't, and is able to think long range."

"Alton is in tune with his feelings, both positive and negative. He knows what bothers him and what gets in his way. He told me once that he used to seek public recognition for almost everything he did. He used to stew about it, until a mentor pointed out that a leader's role is to give recognition to others. He knew it wasn't helping him, and he was able to let go of the need for it."

"If Alton gets frustrated, he seems to notice before we do and does something about it. We never have to deal with it because he is amazingly quick about somehow funneling it into something helpful."

* Scores are on the 1- to 6-point scale (1=never and 6=always) from the 360° Refined™ test. Scores represent the average rating received from all who rated the executive. Scores and coworker comments are from actual people, though names and other identifying information have been altered.

Saakshi R.
Self-awareness score = 5.8

What people who work with her say:
"Saakshi is very adept at knowing what her strengths are as a leader. She knows how she is reacting to something, and adapts her style for maximum effect. She's got a big personality, and I've seen her tone it down without losing who she is altogether."

"No matter what is going on with Saakshi, she can always explain where she's coming from and move the conversation forward. She's a straight shooter, she's honest, and I think people appreciate her for that. They never take what she's saying to them personally."

"When Saakshi faces a challenge at work, she's so aware and open about what she is feeling, more than other execs I've worked for. She's really honest about what she is going through and how things look from her perspective."

What a Lack of Self-awareness Looks Like

Terry N.
Self-awareness score = 1.8

What people who work with her say:

"I wish Terry would be more aware of how her mood affects those around her. She comes across as suspicious of people, as though they do not have the company's best interests at heart. I'm sure she has no idea that she comes across this way, and it makes us feel she doesn't trust us."

"Too often Terry gets caught up in assigning blame rather than understanding her role in creating the issue she's upset about in the first place."

"Terry has no clue about how reckless she is with her comments about directors in front of their peers or employees. She talks about current and past management and shares information about them she should not, or makes derogatory remarks about them. This creates a lack of trust, as you have to wonder what she'll say about you. She has no clue how bad this makes her look."

Hugh P.
Self-awareness score = 2

What people who work with him say:
"When Hugh is feeling stressed, it is felt throughout the department. His mood is palpable around here. I truly believe anything Hugh has done or said is not on purpose or meant to be hurtful; it is just a reaction to the moment and the stress he is feeling."

"Hugh doesn't know his personal limits. He appears to me to be constantly uptight or stressed. He needs to seize opportunities to get away from the rat race to quiet his worries and restore himself because he's dragging everybody else down with him."

"Hugh wears his heart on his sleeve, and does not recognize that his stress level affects others. He needs to realize that everyone is watching him and how he reacts to things as a member of the leadership team."

Self-management

Self-management is what happens when you act—or do not act. It depends on your self-awareness and is the second component of personal competence. Self-management is your ability to use your awareness of your emotions to stay flexible and direct your behavior to positive outcomes. This means managing your emotional reactions to situations and people.

Self-management is more than resisting explosive or problematic behavior. The biggest challenge that leaders face is managing their tendencies over time and applying their self-management skills in various situations. Obvious and momentary opportunities for self-control (e.g., "I'm so mad at my assistant!") are the easiest to spot and manage. Real results come from putting your momentary needs on hold to pursue larger, more important goals. The realization of such goals is often delayed, meaning that your commitment to self-management will be tested repeatedly.

> **Real results come from putting your momentary needs on hold to pursue larger, more important goals.**

Leaders who manage themselves the best are able to see things through without cracking. Success comes to those who can continually manage their tendencies.

Self-management builds upon a foundational skill—self-awareness. Ample self-awareness is necessary for effective self-management because you can choose how to respond to an emotion actively only when you're aware of it and understand it. Since we're hardwired to experience emotions before we can respond to them, it's the one-two punch of reading emotions effectively and then reacting to them that sets the best self-managers apart. The strategies that follow will help you to become one of them.

1. Set the Tone

As a leader, you set the emotional tone in your organization. The behavior you demonstrate—in particular under the influence of strong emotions—primes the emotional state of your people. Expressing positive emotions—in the form of energy, enthusiasm, and a belief in the future—motivates and inspires your people. Expressing negative emotions has the opposite effect. Getting irritable or being down brings other people down with you. When you get jumpy and overreact to things people say and do, your behavior has a negative, contagious effect upon all who witness it. Develop the self-awareness needed to recognize when you are feeling and behaving this way. When you catch yourself doing it, apologize first. Then slow down, remain objective, and model the behavior you want to see in your people.

2. Know the Signs

Self-management requires using awareness of your emotions to choose actively what you say and do. On the surface, it may seem that self-management is simply a matter of taking a deep breath and keeping yourself in check when emotions come on strong. Although it's true that self-control in these situations is a sizeable piece of the pie, there's far more to self-management than putting a cork in it when you're about to blow up. Your eruptions are no different from a volcano—there are all sorts of rumblings happening beneath the surface before the lava starts flowing. Unlike a volcano, you can do subtle things every day to influence what is happening beneath the surface. You just need to learn how to pick up on the rumbling and respond to it. Doing so makes it much easier to manage your emotions.

3. Manage Positive Emotions

If you focus only on negative emotions like anxiety, anger, or irritation, you're missing half the picture when it comes to self-management. Positive emotions need managing, too, especially in business where leaders have a tendency

> **Positive emotions need managing, too, especially in business where leaders have a tendency to think they walk on water when things are going well.**

to think they walk on water when things are going well. Positive emotions can cloud your thinking and lead you to make poor choices just as easily as the negative ones.

4. Sidestep a Hijacking

When you don't stop to think about your feelings (including how they are influencing your behavior now and will continue to do so in the future), you set yourself up to be a frequent victim of emotional hijackings. Whether you're aware of them or not, your emotions will control you, and you'll move through your day reacting to your feelings with little choice in what you say and do. Develop the ability to size yourself up quickly and grab the reins before your emotions hijack your behavior.

5. Make Your Goals Public

Walking your talk is hard, especially when life is always throwing you curveballs. Sometimes, the biggest letdowns are private ones—when we fail to reach a goal or do what we set out to do. There is no more powerful motivator for reaching your

> **Much of self-management comes down to motivation, and you can use the expectations that other people have of you as a powerful force to get you up off the proverbial couch.**

goals than making them public. If you clearly tell other people what you are setting out to accomplish, their awareness of your progress creates an incredible sense of accountability. Much of self-management comes down to motivation, and you can use the expectations that other people have of you as a powerful force to get you up off the proverbial couch.

6. Explore Your Options

Some emotions create a paralyzing fear that makes your thinking so cloudy that the best course of action is nowhere to be found—assuming that there is something you should be doing. In these cases, self-management is revealed by your ability to tolerate the uncertainty as you explore your emotions and options. Once you understand and build comfort with what you are feeling, the best course of action will show itself.

7. Channel Your Emotions into the Behavior You Want

If you're constantly trying to stuff feelings down, you're going to struggle at self-management. Effective self-managers are able to channel emotions into the behavior they want. For example, you can use anxiety and stress about an upcoming deadline to sharpen your focus. Think about what you are feeling and what you need to accomplish, and you'll be surprised how quickly the former helps you achieve the latter.

8. Take Control of Your Self-talk

Research suggests the average person has about 50,000 thoughts every day. There is a strong connection between what you think and how you feel, both physically and emotionally. Our thoughts are "talking" to us every day, and this inner voice is called "self-talk."

When a rush of emotion comes over you, your thoughts can turn the heat up or down. With thoughts being the primary vehicle for regulating your emotional flow, what you allow yourself to think can rumble emotions to the surface, stuff them down underground, and intensify and prolong an emotional experience. By learning to control your self-talk, you can keep yourself focused on the right things and manage your emotions effectively.

A high level of self-management ensures you aren't getting in your own way and doing things that limit your success. It also ensures you aren't frustrating other people to the point that they resent or dislike you. When you understand your own emotions and can respond the way you choose to them, you have the power to take control of difficult situations, react nimbly to change, and take the initiative needed to achieve your goals.

What Self-management Looks Like

Lionel T.
Self-management score = 6*

What people who work with him say:

"I have great respect for an individual who does not 'lose it' in times of adversity. A couple of times things have gone totally wrong, and throughout it all, Lionel channeled his emotions and passion in ways that were constructive. He knew how to inject positive humor into the mix."

"Lionel has great skill in handling himself no matter what the circumstance. He is able to deal with a wide range of employee situations, good and bad, with a calm approach. He possesses a strong ability to communicate under pressure, which garners respect from certain board members! They could learn a few things from Lionel's brand of leadership."

"Lionel is evenhanded and even-tempered in dealing with stress (and he has had a lot of stress lately). I don't know how he does it exactly, but he always seems to find the source of problems and appropriately and effectively resolve them."

---

* Scores are on the 1- to 6-point scale (1=never and 6=always) from the 360° Refined™ test. Scores represent the average rating received from all who rated the executive. Scores and coworker comments are from actual people, though names and other identifying information have been altered.

Yvonne O.
Self-management score = 5.8

What people who work with her say:

"Throughout the many years I have worked with her, I have never seen Yvonne lose her temper, even during major conflicts faced by the teams she's led. I did observe her get mad once during a meeting, but I'm convinced she did it on purpose to grab everyone's attention and get us all to stop and regroup."

"One sign of Yvonne's leadership success is her even-keeled manner in the way she interacts with adversity and handles it adeptly. She creates no emotional drag for the people who work for her."

"Yvonne is a great communicator and remains calm and unflappable in tough situations. During her transition from director to VP, she effectively communicated her goals while maintaining calm, displaying confidence, and including everyone in the process."

What a Lack of Self-management Looks Like

Maritza C.
Self-management score = 1.3

What people who work with her say:
"I wish Maritza would get better at managing her emotions and not fly off the handle. Her mood changes hourly from rational to putting everyone on edge. Sometimes it is like walking on eggshells around here, and to be honest, it's quite stressful. You never know what might send her over the edge."

"One minute Maritza is calm and collected, and then all of a sudden she will become agitated. These episodes are usually triggered by misunderstandings about her instructions. She will get up from her seat several times and raise her voice, directing negative comments at whomever she thinks didn't understand. She does not allow the unlucky targets to speak during these times and often interrupts them when they try. Once she's done saying her piece, she refuses to let anyone rebut or respond in any way. Then she moves on as if nothing has happened!"

"Maritza has a temper and can get very angry and refuse to compromise or back down. I have seen her arguing with people and speaking very disrespectfully—not in keeping with our values. I want Maritza to know that this is seriously hurting her career and advancement because people don't want to work with or for her."

Kyung J.
Self-management score = 2.1

What people who work with him say:

"Kyung needs to slow down, reflect on what needs to be addressed with the person he is speaking to, and provide the most accurate and direct information as possible. When explaining something, he tends to speak quickly and give multiple scenarios, which can be overwhelming and cause people to check out or say they understand something they really don't."

"Sometimes the speed at which Kyung tries to accomplish the work and the speed that he expects from us is too much. He is so bright that he leaves others behind and then gets frustrated that they are not keeping up. His frustration is what turns off the group he is trying to solicit ideas from."

"He should spend a little of his time thinking not only about what he is going to say but also how he is going to say it. Otherwise, I think he will continue to watch people clam up and will continue to get upset. Oftentimes he appears to become so focused on accomplishing his own goals that he doesn't keep the rest of us informed. This will negatively affect our recent commitment at the executive team meeting to get out of our silos."

Social Awareness

As the first component of social competence, social awareness is a foundational skill. Social awareness is your ability to accurately pick up on emotions in other people and understand what is really going on with them. This often means perceiving what other people are thinking and feeling even if you do not feel the same way. It's easy to get caught up in your own emotions and forget to consider the perspective of the other party. Social awareness ensures you stay focused and absorb critical information.

> Social awareness is your ability to accurately pick up on emotions in other people and understand what is really going on with them. This often means perceiving what other people are thinking and feeling even if you do not feel the same way.

Have you ever had your boss approach you, and without saying anything, he or she understood what kind of day you were having and where your mind was wandering? She knew you must have come from a meeting with so-and-so because she could "see it" all over your face. She knew it was probably time to let you vent, instead of asking for that favor she had in mind. She must have picked up on something.

Or how about that waiter who seems to "just know" what each of his customers needs: one couple is in their own world and prefers to be alone; another couple welcomes some fresh conversation from a new person, while another table wants professional and polite service, minus the small talk. Everyone's sitting at a table to eat and drink and be served, and yet there's so much below the surface that makes each table unique. How does he quickly size up these tables and know their needs?

This perceptive leader and waiter have a high level of social awareness, a skill they use to recognize and understand the moods of other individuals and entire groups of people. Though these two may be seasoned veterans at this, it is a skill that they most likely learned and practiced over time. Instead of looking inward to learn about and understand yourself, social awareness is looking outward to learn about and appreciate others. Social awareness is centered on your ability to recognize and understand the emotions of other people. Tuning into others' emotions as you interact with them will help you get a more accurate view of your surroundings, which affects everything from relationships to the bottom line.

> **Tuning into others' emotions as you interact with them will help you get a more accurate view of your surroundings, which affects everything from relationships to the bottom line.**

To build your social awareness skills, you will find yourself observing people in all kinds of situations. You may be observing someone from afar while you're in an airport, or you may be right in the middle of a conversation observing the person to whom you are speaking. You will learn to pick up on body language, facial expressions, posture, and tone of voice. The strategies that follow will help you to increase your social awareness skills.

1. Listen and Observe

Listening and observing are the most important elements of social awareness. To listen well and observe what's going on around us, we have to stop doing many things we like to do. We have to stop talking, stop the monologue that may be running through our minds, stop anticipating the point the other person is about to make, and stop thinking ahead to what we are going to say next. It takes practice to really watch people as you interact with them, to get a good sense of what they are thinking and feeling.

2. Play Anthropologist

At times when you're working on increasing your social awareness, you'll feel like an anthropologist. Anthropologists make their living watching others in their natural state without letting their own thoughts and feelings disturb the observation. This is social awareness in its purest form. The difference is you won't be 100 yards away watching events unfold through a pair of binoculars. To be socially aware, you have to spot and understand people's emotions while you're right there in the middle—a contributing, yet astutely aware, member of the interaction.

3. Pick Up on the Mood in the Room

Emotions are contagious, meaning they spread from one or two people until there's a palpable and collective mood that you can feel at some level. When you enter a room, scan it and notice whether you feel and see energy or quiet, subdued calm. Notice how people are arranging themselves. Are they alone or in groups? Are they talking and moving their hands? Are some more animated than others? What is your gut telling you about them? The sooner you can hone your ability to spot moods in groups, the more skilled you will be as a leader of people.

> **Emotions are contagious, meaning they spread from one or two people until there's a palpable and collective mood that you can feel at some level.**

4. Test Your Accuracy

Even the most socially aware people have off-days or situations they can't quite read. In these cases, there's a social awareness strategy to get the answers you need: just ask. Whether you're a novice or an expert in social awareness, we all need to confirm social observations at some point. The best way to test your accuracy is to simply ask if what you're observing in people or situations is actually what's occurring.

Maybe you have run into Steve at work and noticed that he has a sullen look on his face with his head hanging low and his eyes never looking up from the ground. You ask how he is doing and he says he is doing "just fine." Your evidence is telling you otherwise—he says he's fine, but he doesn't appear to be fine. In this moment, ask a reflective question to clarify what you are seeing. Say something like, "It looks like you are feeling down about something. Did something happen?" Simply stating what evidence you see (*it looks like you are feeling down*) and asking a direct question (*did something happen?*) is a reflective statement at its best.

> **Testing your observations for accuracy will ultimately give you a keener understanding of social situations, and help you pick up on cues that usually fly under the radar.**

You will likely hear whatever he wants you to know for now; but you've reached out to Steve and let him know that you are interested.

Testing your observations for accuracy will ultimately give you a keener understanding of social situations, and help you pick up on cues that usually fly under the radar. If you don't ask, you'll never be certain.

5. Go on a 15-minute Tour

As a leader, you need to be in tune with your people and aware of what's happening around the office. Going on a short tour of the office every day will help you get in tune with other people and their emotions, and refocus your attention on some of the smaller yet critical social cues that exist right under your nose. Things to look for include the look and feel of people's workspaces, the timing of when different people move around the office, and which people seek interaction versus those who are chained to their desks all day. Other people's actions and moods can provide you with critical hints about how things are going collectively.

Like self-awareness, social awareness is a journey rather than a destination. Your goal should be a continual sharpening of the saw so that you maintain the perspective that connects you with your people.

What Social Awareness Looks Like

Arie M.
Social awareness score = 5.9*

What people who work with him say:
"Arie has a knack for connecting emotionally with everyone. He seems to really be able to pick up on what people are feeling. He listens well and offers supportive counsel. He's also a great question-asker."

"He's particularly good at picking up emotional cues from people and tailoring his interactions appropriately. If you're having a bad day, Arie can recognize that and encourage you. He also takes time to get to know people and invest in whoever reports to him. He's been a big encouragement to me."

"Arie has a way of hearing what is really being said, reading the mood of the room, and expressing in words what he feels needs to be said. For example, I was once in a task force meeting, and the group had been slogging through a project for several months. Arie noticed not everyone was engaged and suggested we needed to evaluate who the key stakeholders in the room were to keep moving the

* Scores are on the 1- to 6-point scale (1=never and 6=always) from the 360° Refined™ test. Scores represent the average rating received from all who rated the executive. Scores and coworker comments are from actual people, though names and other identifying information have been altered.

project forward. He framed it that the project focus had changed from its original plan. It gave an opportunity for folks to save face and step down and let others move things forward."

Vivienne Y.
Social awareness score = 5.3

What people who work with her say:
"Vivienne has definitely set herself on the path of becoming a really strong leader. She is very goal oriented, which I appreciate, but she used to be seen as pushy. The new and improved Vivienne pays more attention to what others bring to the table. She has learned that as well as strong opinions, executives bring a lot of emotions into the room. Vivienne now addresses how others on the executive team feel about her goals before setting out on her own course."

"Since last year, Vivienne appears to now understand that by dealing with the reactions of her peers more constructively, her initiatives stay on track, and the others support her rather than fight her or stab her in the back."

"Perception is very important. I am really impressed with what Vivienne has been able to do to turn around how she notices people's responses to what she's saying. Her peers see the progress and appreciate it."

What a Lack of Social Awareness Looks Like

Jim K.
Social awareness score = 2.3

What people who work with him say:

"I wish Jim would get better at communicating at various levels and with different types of people. He could do this through direct contact, and by genuinely inviting and truly listening to others' ideas that may differ from his own. This is really what holds him back from his career aspirations."

"Jim tends to have conversations while looking at his watch, working on the computer, or looking at notes or paperwork while others are talking, giving off signals that he does not value what is being said or who is saying it. He becomes disengaged if what you are saying is not of personal interest to him, unless it involves numbers or profit/loss. It appears to me that he is not really listening or noticing body language, tone, or the emotions of others."

"Jim responds to the words he hears, rather than considering the greater personal impact of what is being discussed. This happens one-on-one and in meetings, and is observed by most who are present. All eyes are on Jim and his actions."

Cheryl D.
Social awareness score = 2.3

What people who work with her say:
"Cheryl lacks sensitivity. She doesn't listen well and speaks when inappropriate. Her delivery style lacks compassion. She isn't approachable and doesn't seem to notice that her audience is disengaged. When other people are speaking, you can tell that she isn't really listening to what they have to say."

"Cheryl puts others down, knowingly or unknowingly. She has a narrow view of how things should be and doesn't deviate from that view. An easy example is I've heard her make comments like, 'It must be nice to go to lunch.' This inadvertently insults the work ethic someone else has without seeking first to understand more about the person, his or her schedule, workload, or commitments."

"I believe that Cheryl really wants the best for people and isn't a mean person, but she really misses the boat when it comes to understanding people. She wants to honor people by giving them freedom, but when she doesn't see things getting done her way she yanks back the power and micromanages. It leaves people feeling misunderstood, chastised, and unable to proceed. I don't see her even noticing or understanding any of this."

Relationship Management

Though relationship management is the second component of social competence, this skill often taps into your abilities in the first three emotional intelligence skills: self-awareness, self-management, and social awareness. Relationship management is your ability to use your awareness of your own emotions and those of others to manage interactions successfully. This ensures clear communication and effective handling of conflict. As a leader, you will find this skill is critical as you work to cultivate relationships across the organization.

Conflicts at work tend to fester when leaders passively avoid problems. This typically happens because leaders lack the skills needed to initiate a direct, yet constructive, conversation. Conflicts at work tend to explode when leaders don't manage their anger or frustration, and choose to take it out on other people. Relationship management gives you the skills you need to avoid both scenarios, and make the most out of every interaction you have with another person.

Conflicts at work tend to fester when leaders passively avoid problems. This typically happens because leaders lack the skills needed to initiate a direct, yet constructive, conversation.

Most people have a spring in their step and put their best foot forward when they are in a new relationship (work or otherwise), but they stumble and lose their footing trying to maintain relationships over the long term. Reality soon sets in that the honeymoon phase is officially over.

The truth is, all relationships take work, even the great ones that seem effortless. We've all heard this, but do we really get it?

Working on a relationship takes time, effort, and know-how. The know-how is emotional intelligence. If you want a relationship that has staying power and grows over time, and in which your needs and the other person's needs are satisfied, the final EQ skill—relationship management—is just what the doctor ordered. The strategies that follow will help you to make it happen.

1. Tap into All of the Emotional Intelligence Skills

Relationship management taps into the three other emotional intelligence skills that you're familiar with—self-awareness, self-management, and social awareness. You use your self-awareness skills to notice your feelings and judge if your needs are being satisfied. You use your self-management skills to express your feelings in a manner that benefits the relationship. Finally, you use your social awareness skills to better understand the other person's needs and feelings.

2. Avoid Giving Mixed Signals

Feelings express truth, and they have a way of rising to the surface through our reactions and body language, despite the words we choose. Telling your staff in a muted voice and frowning face that they did a great job on the product launch (because you're preoccupied with something else) doesn't cut the mustard. People trust what they see over what they hear. Make sure you don't confuse and frustrate others by saying one thing when your body language suggests another.

> **Feelings express truth, and they have a way of rising to the surface through our reactions and body language, despite the words we choose.**

3. Master Stress

Relationship management poses the greatest challenge for most people, especially leaders, during times of stress. When you consider that more than 70% of the people we've tested have difficulty handling stress, it's easy to see why building and sustaining quality relationships poses a challenge for leaders as they maneuver through stressful situations at work. The more stress you're under, the more energy and focus you need to dedicate to your relationships.

4. Quit Winning the Battle to Lose the War

The biggest mistake we see leaders make when it comes to building quality relationships is they go to great lengths to prove that they are right at somebody else's expense. It may feel good in the moment to "win" the interaction, but you're really losing by eroding the quality of the relationship.

5. Model Effective Relationships

In the end, no man is an island, and no leader can do it alone; relationships are an essential and fulfilling part of doing business. They are critical to the success of an organization that is driven by people. Since you set the tone for how relationships are formed in your organization, you are responsible for modeling strong, collaborative relationships. Make effective relationships a priority and watch the effort bear fruit across the organization.

> **Since you set the tone for how relationships are formed in your organization, you are responsible for modeling strong, collaborative relationships.**

6. Tackle Tough Conversations

Tackling tough conversations head-on is a powerful way for leaders to manage relationships effectively. It's essential that you do it and do it well. Whether a staff member is sore at getting passed over for a promotion or team members are in conflict, you need to step up, take the lead, and help everyone maneuver through the problem. Here's how you do it:

i. **Start with agreement.**
   Start the discussion with common ground. Whether simply agreeing that the discussion will be hard but important or agreeing on a shared goal, create a feeling of accord. For example: "Judith, I first want you to know that I value you, and I'm sorry that you learned about the promotion from someone other than me. I'd like to use this time to explain the situation. I'd also like to hear from you."

ii. **Ask the person to help you understand his or her side.**
   People want to be heard—if they don't feel heard, frustration rises. Before frustration enters the picture, beat it to the punch and ask people to share their point of view. Focus on understanding where people are coming from. In Judith's case, this would sound like, "Judith, along the way I want to

make sure you feel comfortable sharing what's on your mind. I'd like to make sure I understand your perspective."

iii. **Resist the urge to plan a "comeback" or a rebuttal.**
Your brain cannot listen and prepare to speak at the same time. In this case, Judith has been passed over for a promotion that she was very interested in and qualified for, and she found out about it through the grapevine. Let's face it—if you'd like to maintain the relationship, you need to be quiet, listen to her shock and disappointment, and resist the urge to defend yourself.

iv. **Help the other person understand your side, too.**
Now it's your turn to help the other person understand your perspective. Describe your thoughts, your ideas, and the reasons behind your actions. Communicate clearly and simply; don't speak in circles or in code. This ability to explain your thoughts and directly address others in a compassionate way during a difficult situation is key to great relationship management.

v. **Move the conversation forward.**
Once you understand each other's perspective, even if there's disagreement, someone has to move things along. In the case of Judith, it's you. Try to find some common ground again. Say something like, "Well, I'm so glad you came to me directly and that we had

the opportunity to talk about it. I understand your position, and it sounds like you understand mine. I'm still invested in your development and would like to work with you on getting the experience you need. What are your thoughts?"

vi. **Keep in touch.**
The resolution to a tough conversation needs attention even after you leave it, so check progress frequently, ask the other person if he or she is satisfied, and keep in touch as you move forward. You are half of what it takes to keep a relationship oiled and running smoothly. Regarding Judith, meeting with her regularly to talk about her career advancement and promotion potential would continue to show her that you care about her progress.

Managing your emotions effectively is fundamental to your success as a leader. Unfortunately, the format of Leadership 2.0 doesn't give us the opportunity to explore emotional intelligence in any more depth than we have in this chapter. If you're looking for additional strategies for improving this critical skill, you should consider reading our other book, Emotional Intelligence 2.0. Emotional Intelligence 2.0 has 66 detailed strategies for improving your emotional intelligence, as well as access to the Emotional Intelligence Appraisal® test, which pinpoints the strategies in the book that will increase your EQ the most.

What Relationship Management Looks Like

Ming C.
Relationship management score = 6*

What people who work with her say:
"Ming is very gifted in personal relationships. She finds out who people are, what makes them tick, and how she can connect with them. It's easy to see how much she values people. This often creates a natural trust between her and everyone who works for her."

"Ming is very strong at relating to team members not just in her department, but across business units. She is well respected because of the relationships that she has built over the years. She represents herself in a manner becoming of our brand."

"She is an extremely friendly person, but Ming does not compromise her work ethic and work responsibilities to be 'friends'; rather, she uses this skill to benefit the collaboration process across the company. She works very well in a matrix environment. She knows how to develop relationships by providing value on her side of the relationship equation and encouraging others to provide value as well."

---

* Scores are on the 1- to 6-point scale (1=never and 6=always) from the 360° Refined™ test. Scores represent the average rating received from all who rated the executive. Scores and coworker comments are from actual people, though names and other identifying information have been altered.

Carl G.
Relationship management score = 5.8

What people who work with him say:

"Carl has terrific relationships with clients. They trust his knowledge and personable consistency over time. In many instances, they act as if Carl works for them. He is especially adept at problem solving. He is able to easily identify and address the root of problems or concerns rather than getting caught up in emotions and negativity. This has a tendency to create a very special bond that translates into client retention."

"Carl quickly gains the trust of people who work for him. He listens well, and has a soft approach when dealing with change and difficult situations. He addresses these things head-on without it becoming an awkward confrontation. This makes him a real asset when dealing with challenges."

"Carl is a genuine, reliable, respectful, and understanding leader. He has the ability to empathize with people and make them trust and believe him. He makes you want to work for him and leads by example."

What a Lack of Relationship Management Looks Like

Anne M.
Relationship management score = 2

What people who work with her say:
"I wish Anne were better with relationships. She tends to talk down to people and doesn't take their needs and desires into consideration. She also doesn't take criticism well, and can be very abrasive when presented with information she doesn't agree with."

"Her peers don't notice the smart and interesting work Anne produces because they have been so badly burned by her unkind words. It worries me that people on the team forget the great contribution that she brings to the team because she has this issue. I encourage her to do what it takes to manage frustration and her relationships more effectively and improve her reputation."

"Anne allows her moods to affect her work and work relationships. At times, she allows her emotions to cloud her objectivity and her treatment of others, which alienates them from her. She can be abrasive and dismissive of others. This has caused a loss of trust among those who report to her or have to work closely with her."

Darius L.
Relationship management score = 1.7

What people who work with him say:
"Darius needs to get to know all of the people who work with and for him on a personal and emotional level. Some feel very comfortable coming and talking to him while others have commented that they don't feel comfortable and connected to him. I believe that this is because relationships have not been built and interactions feel transactional."

"Darius is challenged in building relationships with people and has some social awkwardness. He may mean well or want to, but he seems challenged in building relationships with most of his staff, particularly directors. This disconnect may create lack of trust, less initiative, and resentment among his management team."

"Darius needs to understand the way his actions and words affect the people around him. He can be completely oblivious to the relationship issues he creates with our partners on a day-to-day basis. Darius would be smart to allow others to be experts in their particular area. I truly believe that he thinks he can do everyone's job better than they can. This is not only offensive, but also totally demotivating. Darius could also improve on collaboration. I think he could move the organization ever further forward by rallying different functions to his side."

6
ORGANIZATIONAL JUSTICE

Too few of us are getting what we want from work. We wake up every morning to the sound of the alarm, dress, and rush off only to find ourselves sitting in our cars thinking of other places we would rather be going. On the job, frustrations with colleagues and bureaucracy only intensify these feelings. We spend our downtime thinking of the people we have to put up with, the company we would rather work for, and the futility of work in general.

The highs and lows of work often stem from our interactions with those who have power over us. These individuals make decisions that directly affect our work on a weekly, and often daily, basis. Unfair decisions generate strife. Unheard opinions make us feel resentful and unimportant. Important decisions are made without the input, feedback, or consent of those who will have to live with their impact.

What we are really missing out on at work is organizational justice. Not justice as in equal treatment, the upholding of principles, or conforming to the law, but rather the ability to get what we deserve from the tremendous effort that we put into our work.

Organizational justice is the feeling that your efforts are respected and valued. When you have organizational justice in your work, you know it because you feel empowered, and you close out the day feeling satisfied with how you spent your time.

> When you have organizational justice in your work, you know it because you feel empowered, and you close out the day feeling satisfied with how you spent your time.

If this is the first you've heard of organizational justice, you're missing out on an important movement. Organizational justice is a breakthrough method of understanding work and its impact upon people. Organizational justice enables adaptive leaders and organizations to create an environment that is empowering and ensures there is meaning and purpose in work.

The academic community has long known that organizational justice boosts employee job satisfaction and productivity. When our consultants step inside an organization that's ailing, more often than not they find a lack of organizational justice is either causing or exacerbating the problems there.

For those who lead others, power comes with responsibility—a leader cannot count on his or her employees to create justice for themselves. Understanding this is critical because your people want something more valuable than money for their investment of time and energy in their work. People want to make an impact. Most leaders are not blind to the lack of justice inside their organizations; they simply lack a framework for discussing justice and a method for providing organizational justice to their people.

A lack of organizational justice is the monkey on the back of nearly anyone working inside a large organization. By learning to understand and create organizational justice, you can be a powerful force of change for those who have yet to experience it. Creating organizational justice for your people does not require you to change your organization's structure or philosophy. The only thing you need to change to create justice is yourself.

> **A lack of organizational justice is the monkey on the back of nearly anyone working inside a large organization.**

As a leader, you have direct control over the work environment that your employees experience. Creating justice in that environment is quite possibly the single greatest thing you can do to improve their performance and job satisfaction. So much of what your people experience is a result of the organization they work for, but making things better for your employees is almost entirely up to you. Given the importance of organizational justice to your performance as a leader and the impact of organizational justice upon your people, it is critical you learn how to create it inside your organization.

Organizational justice likely sounds elusive at this point in our exploration, but it is the culmination of three simple skills you can use every day in your work: decision fairness, information sharing, and outcome concern. These skills create justice by giving employees a voice in the decision-making process, sharing information with them, and showing genuine concern for the impact of the decisions made.

Decision Fairness

Your actions set the tone for your employees' work. Every decision you make is important because it trickles down to everyone you lead. The decisions you make do not have to be fair to create justice. Decision fairness is a simple—albeit counterintuitive—method for approaching your decision making that ensures people feel respected and their input is valued.

Most leaders are adept at making quick decisions that maximize results based on the information they have in front of them. However, few leaders are very good at communicating before, during, and after the decision-making process. Leaders forget or underestimate how much the people around them need to feel part of the decision, even when they aren't able to be the one to make the choice. Blindsiding people with the outcome of a decision sends a message that they are not valued.

> **Blindsiding people with the outcome of a decision sends a message that they are not valued.**

When an organization makes a large or small decision, this rarely happens without employees eventually getting wind of how that decision was made. If they feel the process was unfair, they become dissatisfied and unmotivated. You can create decision fairness by committing to doing the following three things consistently and visibly every time you make an important decision:

1. Inform your staff about the upcoming decisions that will affect them.

Most leaders avoid this step because they don't want to disappoint people with the lack of influence they can exert over the decision. Instead, people feel less blindsided by the decisions they have little control over when they know ahead of time that these decisions are going to be made. How you make decisions is just as important as the outcome of your decisions. People want to have a say in what happens to them at work. Letting them know what's coming down the pipe is an important first step in this process.

2. Give employees a voice in matters that will affect them before reaching your decisions, even if you may not be able to use their input.

Equality is not realistic in the world of work. Though some of your people would like to see everyone treated equally, most understand the limits you face when making decisions. Most leaders don't realize this, and they shy away from seeking input from their staff before making a decision.

Create systems that give your employees a voice and gather their input. Let people interact with decision makers through town hall meetings, road shows, and breakfast briefings. Listening to employees is effective because it influences their reaction to a decision regardless of the outcome. Research shows that listening to employees' opinions before making an unfavorable decision greatly improves how they feel about that decision. Listening early also shows you which issues should be addressed carefully when communicating the decision later.

3. When appropriate, use people's input when you make decisions that will affect them.

This is much easier to do when you make the time to do steps 1 and 2 and gather employee input. Most leaders fail this step because they don't feel they have the time to gather input, or they consider decision making the tough but lonely responsibility assigned to them when they took the job. Justice is about empowering people and making their ideas feel valued. You can't do that when you make decisions without considering your employees' valuable input.

If you use a consistent and fair procedure for making decisions, you will see how quickly this has a positive impact upon your employees. Twenty-five years of research shows that decision fairness improves employee job satisfaction, organizational commitment, and job performance.

> **Twenty-five years of research shows that decision fairness improves employee job satisfaction, organizational commitment, and job performance.**

What Decision Fairness Looks Like

Les M.
Decision fairness score = 5.7*

What people who work with him say:

"Les is very good at gathering consensus in a manner that makes others feel good about the situation, even if they don't completely agree. I think he is able to do this because he is clear, direct, open minded, inclusive, and fair. These qualities cause people to have a lot of respect for, and trust in, his recommendations."

"Les explains himself clearly. He's willing to listen to others and gather their input, but presents the company's side of things very fairly and communicates expectations well. He works well with others and often solicits advice and suggestions when making decisions. He's definitely a leader I try to emulate."

"Les takes ownership of complex decisions and is always able to effectively see what people think and communicate to others the information necessary to anticipate and account for concerns or ideas they might have."

---

* Scores are on the 1- to 6-point scale (1=never and 6=always) from the 360° Refined™ test. Scores represent the average rating received from all who rated the executive. Scores and coworker comments are from actual people, though names and other identifying information have been altered.

Gwen W.
Decision fairness score = 5.8

What people who work with her say:

"Gwen is a great leader. She engages each team member during the decision-making process and recognizes and values each member as an expert in his or her respective area. She always actively looks for feedback from team members and gives credit for the feedback when it is ultimately incorporated into a decision. She is great at making everyone feel like a valued, important member of the team."

"Gwen is always fair, open, and honest. She is always very approachable and makes time whenever you need her. She seeks others' opinions and takes them into consideration when making decisions that affect them."

"Gwen is excellent at considering all aspects of a problem and making fair decisions that allow employees to give input and understand the reasons for the decisions."

What a Lack of Decision Fairness Looks Like

Kevin H.
Decision fairness score = 1.8

What people who work with him say:

"When making decisions, Kevin doesn't take into account the impact they'll have on all involved parties. He should seek other groups' input, be open to collaboration from the beginning of a project, and practice over-communication. For example, instead of discussing database builds solely with the outside consulting group, he could have involved the operations group that had been doing the implementing. Both groups could have worked together up front toward the best solution."

"There are too many occasions when Kevin demonstrates hidden agendas or uses favoritism to make decisions. This is made worse by using fear tactics to motivate people to follow decisions we were left out of. His positive side gets completely overshadowed because of this. Kevin should realize that we are a team. I feel only a special group of people are considered to be the team. Just look at his recent promotion decisions. Promotions should be earned, not just given to friends. He has to include us all to develop a strong team and to continue the success and growth of the business."

"Kevin needs to better understand the impact of his decisions by doing a thorough overview of issues/opportunities before making the decision. He often lacks facts and does not truly provide an opportunity for input or sharing."

Kim R.
Decision fairness score = 1.4

What people who work with her say:
"When decisions are made that add to workloads, Kim never addresses what we consider giant issues. She doesn't explain why the decision was made or how we factored into the decision. For example, many people were upset because a project was going in one direction and has now drastically changed to another direction. They were worried that the work being requested was unrealistic and extreme, and she never explained to them the importance of the change, or how it was a much better direction for the project."

"I thought Kim was selected because she was so adept at navigating cultural complexities, but she blew it with the way she handled the cuts in Singapore. She was very upset that such a large group of reverential people were so vocal in their displeasure with her actions. But Kim deserved to have egg on her face. Her call for them to be 'loyal' to the company because it was going through tough times fell flat because she fired 300 people without consulting anyone.

Naturally, people were upset by this, and they were not afraid to show it. The way Kim handled this decision is having a massive, negative impact upon morale there."

"It's obvious that Kim has her favorites here. The decisions that get made for one region should go for everyone. It's not fair to us to go to another region and find that it's okay for them to do something we cannot. Right now it seems like there's a double standard, and nothing has been explained."

Information Sharing

When justice is lacking, information does not flow freely. Ideas are guarded, and employees are uncertain about what will happen next. Decisions are reached without input and delivered without warning. Most leaders aren't malicious or manipulative in withholding information. They're just too busy or blind to grasp the importance that employees place on gaining access to information.

The companies people work for can feel like a giant bulldozer tearing a path. Their choice is to get out of the way, or if they are lucky, hitch a ride. Either option does not give people the opportunity to take the controls. However, an organization that is fair or "just" explains to their employees the path they are taking and why. This is what you can do as an adaptive leader. This information could be as significant as explaining the reasons behind a reorganization, or as small as having managers explain how they chose to assign individuals to project teams. The result of all this explaining is a feeling of satisfaction in employees that boosts productivity.

Leaders who get people to love their jobs do so by being good stewards of information. As a leader, you can easily take for granted the access you have to information. Sharing this information freely and ensuring everyone stays in the

> **Leaders who get people to love their jobs do so by being good stewards of information.**

loop empowers people. There are limits of course, but with discretion, the rule should be "share more information, not less." Justice ensures that information flows in two directions so that employees feel heard and they clearly understand the movements of the organization.

How information is shared is also highly important. A memo or an email is often confusing for employees and seen as cold or manipulative. Employees value when information is shared in a format in which they can discuss the implications and ask questions. You never know how employees will react to a decision or how they will perceive the information shared. Therefore, it is essential that information is delivered in a format where questions and concerns can be voiced.

To create a fair and just climate through the skill of information sharing, you need to commit to doing just two things consistently and visibly:

1. Explain to employees how and why decisions were made that affect them, regardless of whether you were the one who made the decision.

Withholding the rationale behind a decision has a negative impact on employee morale even when employees think the decision was fair. The key to creating justice is to share the information you have whenever you can. Schedule time to sit down with employees and have a discussion. Explain why and how a decision was made. Even a discussion about why there is information you are not sharing shows respect and provides people with information. The knowledge you impart places people in a more informed, aware position, and creates a tangible sense that they are valued.

> **Withholding the rationale behind a decision has a negative impact on employee morale even when employees think the decision was fair.**

Any excess time people spend waiting for an explanation is time spent in angst and dissatisfaction. This discontent is exacerbated when employees do not understand the rationale for a decision. Leaders often withhold the rationale for a decision because they think it won't help the situation any to share this information. The great thing about organizational justice is employees do not need to agree with a decision for sharing information to benefit them. Your employees can see through their own needs—they understand that an organization must make decisions to ensure the livelihood of the entity even when the decision benefits some more than others.

2. Thoroughly discuss the impact decisions made will have on people.

If you don't take the time to talk through how the repercussions of decisions will impact everyone (including providing ample opportunity for people to ask questions), then you've left out critical information. People want to understand the fallout, big or small, from change, and you show tremendous respect as a leader by taking the time to explore this fallout together.

Research shows that the mere presence of a sincere explanation positively influences employee reactions to unfavorable circumstances. When employees know what is going on and why, they are far more apt to be understanding and contented.

What Information Sharing Looks Like

Jake L.
Information-sharing score = 5.9*

What people who work with him say:
"Jake is good at communicating with employees promptly. He is open to listening to information from all. I think he is great at explaining why things are done. For example, he often shares the history of or reason for making a decision or taking an action."

"He sees the value in his team and treats them as equals not beneath him or pawns in the game. Jake also takes time to communicate with everyone no matter what position he or she has in the company. He is brilliant at simplifying complex situations and informing staff of decisions that impact them. He checks in with people outside his department to make sure that they feel supported and encouraged."

"Jake is very approachable and willing to spend time explaining and discussing all aspects of a business situation. For example, he discussed at length an issue regarding the decisions about our research center, explaining the decision

---

* Scores are on the 1- to 6-point scale (1=never and 6=always) from the 360° Refined™ test. Scores represent the average rating received from all who rated the executive. Scores and coworker comments are from actual people, though names and other identifying information have been altered.

process and spending time soliciting comments and questions even though he was under a tremendous time constraint."

Eileen K.
Information-sharing score = 5.7

What people who work with her say:
"Eileen makes sure everyone understands situations outside his or her own area. She does this by recapping conversations or information for everyone at different levels, which creates a common understanding. This allows everyone to be able to give feedback and feel confident his or her opinion counts."

"Eileen is a fantastic explainer of information. The amount of ease with which she grasps interconnected activities is staggering. Sometimes we just need to hear it from her."

"Eileen is a strong leader. She is a good communicator when her employees ask her for advice. She shares appropriate information with her employees, listens to their thoughts on decisions, and informs them of possible outcomes based on her experience."

What a Lack of Information Sharing Looks Like

Adam L.
Information-sharing score = 1.3

What people who work with him say:
"Adam is very bad at communicating with his immediate staff. We rarely feel like we are up to date with information needed to perform our jobs at a high level. Most of the time we are left to make plans on our own, only to find out that plans have changed."

"Adam seems to withhold information until divulging it suits his needs. I believe he would gain others' support more quickly if they trusted they were being told everything up front. He should remember that he is part of an organization, and that other people need information he has."

"I wish Adam handled information better. He withholds a lot from the staff and refers to the project deliverables as his personal achievements. He does not delegate responsibilities and avoids including others in project deliverables in an effort to obtain personal recognition."

Rochelle V.
Information-sharing score = 2.2

What people who work with her say:

"I think that Rochelle can become better at taking the initiative to communicate information to people when it is critical to a project. She seems to communicate only what she knows when she's asked to do so. At that point, she's very informative."

"She tends to assume that others know what's behind decisions without communicating it. And when she's asked, she seems to be insulted because she assumes everyone knows she's got it under control. In most cases, it is under control. In others, it's not even close."

"Rochelle does not communicate why decisions were made, her global vision and plan, her expectations of us, or feedback on performance. She should disseminate information she is privy to in order to improve the job performance of everyone involved."

Outcome Concern

Most people are happiest at work when they feel they make a difference and have a sense of purpose. In an unjust environment, employees find themselves going unnoticed and feeling stuck in a dead-end job where they have no impact. When employees leave these situations, they are not leaving jobs—they are leaving bosses who don't care about them (or don't appear to care).

> **When employees leave these situations, they are not leaving jobs— they are leaving bosses who don't care about them (or don't appear to care).**

To create a climate of organizational justice, you must have compassion for how decisions impact your people, and you have to find ways to demonstrate this compassion consistently and visibly—a skill called outcome concern. There are three steps to demonstrating outcome concern:

1. Express sincere concern for your employees when you share decisions that affect them.

To show your compassion for any unfavorable circumstances that will result from a decision, you have to meet people where they are at. Most leaders are prone to action and are uncomfortable "wallowing" in a situation that no one can change. Your employees don't see it this way. When you show your people that you truly understand and care about

> **Most leaders are prone to action and are uncomfortable "wallowing" in a situation that no one can change.**

how the decision impacts them, you show that you respect and value them rather than making them upset you don't do something about it.

2. Check in with your staff regarding their reactions to decisions that affect them.

Whether it's a group meeting or you sit down one-on-one, be sure to ask your staff to share their reactions and feelings about the decision and then share yours. When difficult decisions must be made, checking in with your staff shows your emotional investment in the experience of those affected by the decision. Leaders who show real concern for the impact of decisions by asking thoughtful questions quickly become the ones everyone wants to work for.

3. Teach management to do the same.

The managers who report to you must demonstrate outcome concern as well, or this will derail your efforts. Teach your managers why organizational justice is important and how you are making a commitment to it. Specific skills can be built through effort, but that won't happen until your managers understand how committed you are to creating an environment of organizational justice. Your managers need to see you demonstrate the same skills you're asking of them, and they need to be held accountable for demonstrating these skills. Tell them why justice is a priority to you and the organization. Be certain to seek their feedback regarding how justice should be implemented in the organization.

If you haven't considered the power of including your staff before, during, and after decisions, get started by taking the time to discuss a recent decision. As you increase the level of organizational justice for your employees, they will become more committed to you and the organization.

What Outcome Concern Looks Like

Stuart W.
Outcome concern score = 5.6*

What people who work with him say:

"Stuart has a way of helping people see the changes that the company needs to make in a clear and caring way. He always uses humor when appropriate to lift the mood and schedules time where everyone can think through and talk about the ripple effects. The benefit plan discussion is a great example."

"Stuart can analyze a complicated situation and provide simple explanations that make sense to people. Stuart also takes a personal interest in his people and makes them feel cared for."

"Stuart inspires confidence in his staff. When he makes decisions that will affect us, he listens to our stance and takes great care to explain the repercussions of the decision. He accepts responsibility for the success or failures of his decisions and cares how we feel about it."

---

* Scores are on the 1- to 6-point scale (1=never and 6=always) from the 360° Refined™ test. Scores represent the average rating received from all who rated the executive. Scores and coworker comments are from actual people, though names and other identifying information have been altered.

Maria G.
Outcome concern score = 5.7

What people who work with her say:
"Morale has jumped significantly in Maria's department since her arrival. She is a great communicator, which was very much needed when she arrived. She quickly earned the respect of her employees and peers due to her caring attitude and genuine interest in their welfare."

"Maria is very dedicated to her job, the company, and her staff, and goes above and beyond the call of duty. She cares about results and, at the same time, cares about her employees. She's really good at bringing those two together even when employees have to adjust to changes being made."

"Maria often hosts webinars, inviting all who wish to attend, on what's going on across the company and what's going on in the industry. This is a great tool for bringing her department together and answering questions. It shows she really cares about us. I believe more of these can only help morale, communication, and commitment."

What a Lack of Outcome Concern Looks Like

Holly M.
Outcome concern score = 1.7

What people who work with her say:

"Holly has difficulty communicating that she cares about other people and values what they do for the firm. The shame of this is that I think caring for others is one of her values; she just does not communicate it well."

"Many of the people in the office do not feel that Holly appreciates them. This is mostly due to the way they were treated in her first six months here. Holly often speaks of goals and initiatives from the company's viewpoint. I think she would get more buy-in if she made more effort to state goals and initiatives from the viewpoint of her employees."

"Holly seems to believe that anything that the firm develops is perfect, and should be put into place immediately. She doesn't seem to care how this affects us or our interactions with our clients."

Saul G.
Outcome concern score = 1.0

What people who work with him say:
"Saul needs to become a better listener and show more genuine concern, rather than worrying about himself. When I have approached him about concerns about salary, quotas, additional travel, etc., he has always responded to my concerns by talking about himself and shows no concern for me. This has created an atmosphere in which I keep things to myself, knowing that Saul won't listen and probably doesn't care unless it is affecting him and his bottom line."

"When dealing with decisions that affect employees and the departments, Saul doesn't seem to understand the impact of waiting weeks to make the decision. He also doesn't seem concerned with what we think about it."

"I would like to tell him that anytime he's dealing with decisions that affect our employees with negative outcomes, the issue can't be handled slowly or in a terse, non-caring manner."

7
CHARACTER

The minute you step into a leadership role, you take on a rarely discussed and often taxing responsibility. You become the mechanism by which your organization breathes life and connects with its people. Every day you balance being human (talented and flawed) with serving as the most visible vessel for the organization. As you inspire, mobilize, and make decisions, you embody your organization's goals, methods, and culture. You also embody your life experience, beliefs, and values. It can get tricky to represent the organization well and still be yourself. Leadership requires that you strive for both. Otherwise, you will limit what you can achieve, weaken the organization, disappoint the people relying on you, and even lose yourself in the process. Leadership challenges build character, and adaptive leaders make sure the character they build is sound.

> **Leadership challenges build character, and adaptive leaders make sure the character they build is sound.**

Character is a cohesive approach to conducting yourself, interacting with others, and representing the organization.

Character is built over time through integrity, credibility, and valuing differences (acting on the belief that everyone has something to offer). The leadership challenges that will build your character are almost always complicated dilemmas or difficult decisions. As Abraham Lincoln put it, "Nearly all men can stand adversity, but if you want to test a man's character, give him power." When you successfully pass tests of character, you strengthen your people's relationship with and loyalty to your organization. If you fail, those working for you can't reach their potential. It's never too late to build your character. Your people and your organization are counting on it.

> **As Abraham Lincoln put it, "Nearly all men can stand adversity, but if you want to test a man's character, give him power."**

Integrity

To be understood as a leadership skill, integrity has to be looked at through a practical lens. Integrity is the consistency between what you say, what you do, what you value, and what the organization values. Employees typically talk about a leader's integrity only when it's either strikingly absent, a standout moment, or after the fact (at your retirement party). On a day-to-day basis, they may not be asking for it the way they ask for updates in a staff meeting, but make no mistake about it. Integrity is always there as a "to do" written in permanent invisible ink.

People expect you to do the right thing. They want you to operate with integrity all the time and everywhere you go. Yet they won't and shouldn't have to spell out what integrity looks like for you. You will have to do that for yourself.

Integrity becomes elusive when we rush around with a "get things done" mindset to the exclusion of the "how am I getting things done" mindset. Adaptive leaders think at a deeper level about how their actions or words are out of sync with their own values, their people's values, and the company's values. They are self-correcting while getting things done; they mold their approach over many difficult lessons and move toward an intangible "right" way.

The strategies that follow capture the invisible "to dos" for building integrity and gaining it back when you've allowed it to slip away under pressure.

1. Walk Your Talk

Leaders who don't walk their talk stand out like a sore thumb. Strive for consistency with what you say and do in a way that resonates with what you believe to be important. Your behavior should reflect the things you say are important to you and to the organization. Consider your dealings with others to be your platform for projecting and demonstrating integrity. Emails and voicemails, hallway and elevator conversations, golf games, press conferences, company picnics, staff meetings, and boardroom presentations—they all matter because your people are watching you.

2. Never Place Self-interest First

People can spot it a mile away when you put your personal goals above the organization's goals. You are leading your organization. If you win at your organization's expense, you become a liability. Just read the headlines covering notorious business fiascos, and you will see leaders who used power for personal gain. Don't become one of them.

> **People can spot it a mile away when you put your personal goals above the organization's goals.**

3. Don't Lose Yourself

Typically, leaders have no problem standing behind their organization's vision and priorities. This becomes a problem when you lose or compromise yourself in the process. Speak up for what you need and believe in (family balance, honesty, etc.) to ensure your personal and professional integrity align.

4. Take a Good Look at Yourself

Take a good hard look at what you've been doing lately, how people are responding to it, and where you can better align who you are with who the organization needs you to be. If you can't find opportunities for improvement through this process, then you aren't being honest with yourself. Repeating this process at year's end is a great way to take stock annually to produce fruitful insights and possibilities for recommitting to what's really important to you.

5. Be a Good Steward

Leaders with integrity have a strength of character that motivates them to put their people first. They ignore self-interest and personal gain to serve the larger group. Leaders who are good stewards are authentic and straightforward in their dealings with others. They do what they promise, and are guided by a clear set of convictions. Their values are rarely compromised because, like a shepherd guarding a flock, protecting their people is their highest priority.

> **Leaders with integrity have a strength of character that motivates them to put their people first.**

6. Live without Regrets

At the end of the day as you're heading home, you need to know that you said what needed to be said and did what needed to be done. You must know that your actions weren't dictated by your circumstances—they were dictated by your integrity. If they weren't, tomorrow should have a new priority at the top of your list. It's never too late to bring something up when your integrity is at stake. Lead with integrity, and you'll have no regrets.

Leading with integrity requires you keep yourself on the right track. Your integrity can provide you with a protective barrier against those forces that will compromise what's most important to you, your people, and your organization.

What Integrity Looks Like

Gordon W.
Integrity score = 6*

What people who work with him say:
"Gordon is a great leader. He inspires trust and friendship. People like working with him. He has a good heart and cares about doing the right thing. I admire the way he handles himself when faced with adversity: with pride and integrity."

"Gordon is the consummate professional who holds himself and his people to very high standards. His actions support his ideals. In addition, he backs up this ethic with his willingness to reach out directly to his team and his customers. Gordon is a go-to person for new initiatives and gives his all, whether it directly benefits his own business unit or the larger organization."

"Gordon is a motivational leader who really listens to others and encourages their success. He will never stab someone in the back to further his own goals. He is competitive, but not so much that he will step on others to get ahead. He is someone people look up to and want to do well for. He is

---

* Scores are on the 1- to 6-point scale (1=never and 6=always) from the 360° Refined™ test. Scores represent the average rating received from all who rated the executive. Scores and coworker comments are from actual people, though names and other identifying information have been altered.

principled and trustworthy, and puts the good of the group over personal gain."

Sharika C.
Integrity score = 5.7

What people who work with her say:
"Sharika is a woman of integrity. She is always approachable and strives to work through a problem for the best results. She takes an ethical stand with difficult problems and touchy issues that might cast a bad light on the organization."

"I appreciate her desire to do the right thing to develop the organization and to create a professional and civil environment. Sharika accepts responsibility for the success or failures of her decisions without hoarding glory or casting blame."

"Sharika has a very high level of integrity and always ensures that she's doing everything with both the work and the people in mind. I see her trying hard to balance moving the organization forward while at the same time ensuring her working relationships are intact."

What a Lack of Integrity Looks Like

Alicia R.
Integrity score = 2

What people who work with her say:

"Alicia doesn't integrate her work and personal ethics. She needs to become a model of integrity. Right now she doesn't speak honestly and doesn't act with the best intentions for everyone involved. I really don't think she has an honest bone in her body. She isn't reliable in any circumstance, so I don't trust her no matter who she's talking to or in what sort of a situation."

"Alicia doesn't display being the same on the inside as she claims to be on the outside. I believe she's failing to become a leader because she demonstrates a poor level of integrity. She puts on a false illusion of leadership in front of her team, but after the show is over, when she's away from the spotlight, her conduct is anything but inspirational."

"This office's productivity has little to do with Alicia. Although she does care about making the division successful, sometimes she cares more about promoting herself and her chosen few. The difficult economy makes some employees stay, but you will not hear the occasional happy chatter in this office like before she was promoted."

Gerard P.
Integrity score = 1.7

What people who work with him say:

"Gerard has no integrity. He talks about almost everyone behind his or her back. When things do not work out his way, he does everything possible to kick people out, no matter what it takes. He is after meeting his own goals, not the company's or team's goals. He has no respect for his senior staff."

"He needs to treat others the way he wants to be treated. Gerard has to remember he sets an example. He's on the ethics committee, and he practices the opposite of what he preaches. He just isn't the professional I expected of our leader."

"Gerard isn't very consistent between what he says is important to him (the company's priorities) and what his actions suggest are important to him (his own glory). I can't figure out what he stands for underneath all the bravado."

Credibility

Leaders who have credibility provide a voice of authority. The weight of this authority stems from how much people value what you offer (what you know, who you are, and how you conduct yourself). Credibility is a combination of what you bring with you from your past and what you're doing with it in the present. You can have credibility as the person who knows the relevant facts, but no credibility as a person who knows how to deal with people and vice versa. What you know (expertise in your field), who you are (understanding your own strengths and style), and how you conduct yourself (your treatment of others) each contribute to your credibility as a leader.

> You can have credibility as the person who knows the relevant facts, but no credibility as a person who knows how to deal with people and vice versa.

Credible leaders earn people's trust because they contribute something extremely valued when it really matters, like expertise, sound advice, extra support, or a welcome opinion. They've been there and done that, so people around them listen hard when a credible source speaks up or takes a stand. It may sound counterintuitive, but there is a definite risk of overdoing it. No one likes working for a know-it-all or a boss who steals the limelight.

Credibility is gained over time when you contribute just what people need. Comedians say they are only as funny as their last joke, and leaders are only as credible as their recent actions or words would suggest. If your bio is packed with impressive degrees, but that stance you took in today's meeting doesn't hold water, your credibility can sink.

Adaptive leaders take steps in three areas to build their credibility: 1) what they know, 2) who they are, and 3) how they operate. Here are six important steps that will help you increase your credibility:

1. Earn It

Credibility is built in small doses over time. If you really want to be perceived as credible, you have to put the time in to earn it bit by bit, day by day. Unfortunately, credibility is one of those tricky things that leaders can lose in an instant. So, if you want to be perceived as credible, you better make sure this is really important to you. Otherwise, you'll never put enough work in to see it happen.

> **Credibility is built in small doses over time. If you really want to be perceived as credible, you have to put the time in to earn it...**

2. Let Your Actions Speak

If you're asking the people in your organization to go the extra mile, then you better be doing the same. Don't ask the CIO and his team to miss out on the holidays to handle a crisis if you're heading to the islands to bask in the sun. You don't have to be a programmer to stick around—they'll appreciate the support, leadership, and recognition your presence provides. The mixed messages you send when you leave your people in the lurch absolutely destroy your credibility.

3. Speak Their Language

If you're in a leadership position, you already know that leading doesn't require you to be an expert in everything. You do have to know enough to make sound decisions commensurate with your leadership level and industry. If people are telling you that your leadership is weak because you don't have an accounting background, they really mean you don't know enough about basic accounting issues or you aren't effectively tapping into the expertise of your accounting staff. Sometimes you need to buckle down and broaden your expertise a bit. Attend an executive seminar, hop online and work through a series of Khan Academy lessons, find an expert to coach you, or read everything you can get your hands on until you are credible enough to speak the same language as the rest of your team.

4. Be Reliable and Consistent

To maintain credibility, you have to follow through on what you say you will do. Even if you are an expert in your field, you won't have much credibility if you are unreliable or unavailable, or your behavior is all over the map. As with integrity, you must demonstrate consistency in your words and deeds to establish true credibility.

5. Know When to Keep Your Mouth Shut

Leaders don't always have the right answer, and leaders who reek of credibility know how to use their silence effectively. They know when to listen and ask good questions. Consider yourself a seeker of valuable insight, ideas, and answers. To gather intelligence, you can't be talking all the time.

6. Distinguish the Forest from the Trees

Leaders tend to know something about a lot of things and a lot about a few things. In your quest to lead with credibility, don't fool yourself into thinking that you have to know everything about everything. That's what the great people who work for you are there for. Instead, keep your eye on the horizon and tap into

> **In your quest to lead with credibility, don't fool yourself into thinking that you have to know everything about everything.**

those who know the specifics when you need them. Your responsibility is to know where the answers lie and mobilize people to produce them.

There are two aspects of credibility you may find frustrating. First, you can't create it quickly across the board. Sometimes you will be considered credible by one group, but remain an outsider with another. Give your credibility the time it needs to grow. Second, other people get to decide when you are credible, not you. People need to catch you taking credible actions; then they will be the ones to spread the word.

What Credibility Looks Like

Young-Soo M.
Credibility score = 5.7*

What people who work with him say:

"Young-Soo builds solid relationships based on credibility and trust. He has high ethical standards and can be counted upon to make sound decisions on behalf of the company. He is a pleasure to work with."

"He is a no-nonsense, results-oriented individual with excellent presence and credibility. Young-Soo is true to his engineering background and makes intelligent decisions based on fact. He is a trustworthy executive and always walks his talk."

"Young-Soo is a great leader. He has the utmost respect from his team and the other development teams he works with. He provides strong direction and valuable insight, and is open and seeks input and feedback from all stakeholders. Young-Soo has been a great partner and is incredibly valued and trusted by me, by our leadership, and by our board. We are fortunate to have his experience, vision, sensibilities, and credibility."

---

* Scores are on the 1- to 6-point scale (1=never and 6=always) from the 360° Refined™ test. Scores represent the average rating received from all who rated the executive. Scores and coworker comments are from actual people, though names and other identifying information have been altered.

Kaatje P.
Credibility score = 5.5

What people who work with her say:
"Kaatje is a top-quality individual. She has an outstanding moral character and can be counted on to accomplish the toughest assignments. She is great at making her employees feel appreciated. She makes good, sound decisions, and takes input from others. Kaatje's very straightforward, credible, honest, and fact-based in her arguments. She does not tolerate office politics. Her people would follow her off a cliff if she so desired."

"In the face of adversity, Kaatje can always be counted on to organize resources, ideas, and techniques to thoroughly explore the issue at hand and identify creative, credible solutions. She has solid leadership and communication skills, and is always quick to highlight the contributions of others, even sometimes minimizing her own contribution so that others can shine."

"Kaatje is someone who can always be counted on to come through in a pinch. Although she is very busy and has a large workload, she is very willing to drop what she is doing to play her part in something that is a last-minute, higher priority. She is also good at setting up boundaries and timelines for others to understand so that they know what they can expect from her. This is why she's so credible when she speaks up."

What a Lack of Credibility Looks Like

Vicente P.
Credibility score = 2.3

What people who work with him say:

"Vicente is not well respected. I don't know if he realizes how much his credibility and trust have been damaged over time with his impulsive comments and decisions. His leaders are working in a silo without his support and just trying to do the best they can to lead their teams, all the while being cautious of where they step. Some have chosen to limit communication as a result."

"Vicente needs to realize that the only way to earn true credibility is to provide timely and useful service to our clients. Giving them what he thinks they need in his own timeframe is ineffective. He needs to solicit what they need and provide immediate and substantive results to gain respect and be a true partner."

"He has good intentions, but Vicente's emotions are his driver. He needs to take a moment before he responds to things to make sure it is the correct response. Doing this consistently might help him regain credibility."

Judy K.
Credibility score = 2

What people who work with her say:

"Judy does not have the trust and respect of her staff. People are afraid to go to her with issues. They feel she places herself above everyone else instead of leading by example. She would earn a great deal of credibility and respect from employees if she would just live by the rules she creates."

"Judy is only concerned with her own interests and will never fight for others, so people don't trust her or back her up. In conversation, she asks questions but rarely listens to the answers. Instead, she speaks while you are speaking because she is not interested in anyone else's views. The way she presents herself and behaves in front of staff prevents her from being respected as a credible, in-charge leader, or even a full professional."

"I would like to see Judy take her role more seriously by being more consistent. She is technically a leader by her position title, but cannot be counted on as credible by the other execs or staff. Her lack of follow-through allows others to do what they want and take advantage."

Values Differences

More often than not, the message a leader hears in a confidential session with an executive coach sounds something like this: "What you can accomplish now and in the future has everything to do with what you can accomplish through others. It's just not about you anymore." Leaders who aren't privy to this guidance early enough in their careers head down one of three possible paths: 1) micromanaging because they don't trust anyone but themselves, 2) trying

> **What you can accomplish now and in the future has everything to do with what you can accomplish through others. It's just not about you anymore.**

to be a superhero by being the only one who can save the day, or 3) trying to be a one-man or one-woman show because they seek all the glory.

Maybe you've worked for one of these leaders. One-man-show types hire weak players, so no one will threaten their prominence. These leaders fear the talents of others. Micromanagers don't believe other people have much to offer and are driven by a disdain for other people's talents. Superheroes see people as mere mortals who couldn't survive without a caped crusader to swoop in and save the day. Superheroes don't trust the capabilities of the people they lead.

Even if you've traveled down these paths a bit yourself, it's time to recommit to valuing all that people have to offer, especially their differences. This way you can build a competitive advantage and reap the rewards that all your people's skills have to offer. The wider the variability of your people's skills, the healthier your organization, and the more adaptable it will be to changes in the marketplace. The strategies that follow will help you value differences and fully capitalize on diverse ideas, skills, and experience.

1. Cure Yourself of Mini-me Syndrome

It's human nature to be drawn to people who remind you of yourself. As a leader you can't allow yourself to get sucked into this mini-me syndrome; it will greatly limit the creativity and capability of your team. Hire, develop, and promote people who bring widely different qualities to the table. Seek out people with unique strengths, different personal styles, and wildly diverse backgrounds. Then seek their advice and counsel on the challenges you face.

2. Value Dissenting Opinions

Adaptive leaders have the courage to embrace the contributions of those whose perspectives challenge them. Dissenting opinions should send you to a screeching halt, ready to listen carefully to what others have to say. You need to create a culture that respects and values dissenting opinions. Start a conversation inside your organization that demonstrates the value of diverse opinions. Add inclusion to your organization's list of values, and measure your supervisors' and managers' demonstration of respect for dissenting opinions and unique perspectives.

> **Dissenting opinions should send you to a screeching halt, ready to listen carefully to what others have to say.**

3. Treat People How They Want to Be Treated

If you're successful in surrounding yourself with people who are very different from you, then you can't treat them the way you would want to be treated. Their methods for communication, time management, and approaching conflict, among others, will be foreign to you. It's your job to pick up on these differences and learn about them by asking good questions and adjusting your approach to working together. This will take some time to get going. You can take steps to foster this process, such as getting to know them over lunch. Your efforts will deepen your working relationships and put in place the chemistry for accomplishing great things together.

4. Remember, You Can't Do It Alone

Yes, it's lonely at the top, but only if you look past everyone around you. Don't believe it when people tell you that success rests on the shoulders of a chosen few. You can do more through others, and the more different they are from you and your team, the more these differences will serve to foster innovation and enhance the quality of your organization.

> **Yes, it's lonely at the top, but only if you look past everyone around you.**

Differences can be a great source of discomfort for many leaders. Embracing differences will build your leadership character. Elevate the differences among your people from problems that need to be managed to resources that are valued. Soon, these differences will become clay you can shape and mold into great results. How well you're able to do this will determine in large part how much you're able to accomplish with your people.

What Values Differences Looks Like

Leticia C.
Values differences score = 5.7*

What people who work with her say:
"Leticia respects every individual and what they bring to the unit. It seems to me she recognizes the differences, strengths, and shortcomings between people and finds ways to work within and around them."

"I sincerely believe that Leticia is fully committed to running an exceptional unit. She recognizes that we are all individuals and we bring to the table different experiences and different methods of achieving the same goals."

"Leticia can see things from others' perspectives and appreciates that perspective. She understands that someone else's approach might be more appropriate."

---

* Scores are on the 1- to 6-point scale (1=never and 6=always) from the 360° Refined™ test. Scores represent the average rating received from all who rated the executive. Scores and coworker comments are from actual people, though names and other identifying information have been altered.

Shaun O.
Values differences score = 5.4

What people who work with him say:

"Shaun is very supportive and easy to get along with. He has great interpersonal skills and allows for individual differences. For example, he knows I prefer more structured protocols, and he is very supportive in my use of these methods."

"Shaun is very fair-minded and makes every effort to see the wide variety in his team. He values what they each have to offer."

"Shaun is great with people. He is intelligent and has an understanding nature, with tremendous respect for differences. He is tolerant of the many challenges that working in a large and complex organization can bring, and is willing to systematically and patiently work through the challenges to bring about a desired result."

What a Lack of Values Differences Looks Like

Phil T.
Values differences score = 1.6

What people who work with him say:

"Phil does not embrace the differences and diversity of staff. He needs to be accepting of who we are, not of who he would like us to be. He should recognize and develop our individual strengths, and try to develop communication skills that are individualized for each team member. He shows no empathy or awareness of his employees' differences and how his employees react to situations."

"Phil needs to acknowledge that all personal contributions are valued regardless of background. He needs to find common ground to leverage the skills we bring to the table, so we can make the best contribution to the business. I don't think he is open to different cultures."

"Respect all team members for what we each bring, and the daily work efforts we make in our areas no matter how great or small these efforts are. Please understand that we want to work with you as allies, not as foes, to achieve our goals. Create a comfortable and safe work atmosphere where there are mutual respect and honest communication, and not an atmosphere of doubt."

Colleen S.
Values differences score = 1.7

What people who work with her say:
"Colleen doesn't see the potential in others. She just thinks it's her way or the highway. She should be open to new points of view, and take the time to recognize opportunities to collaborate. She is way too focused on herself."

"She rarely appreciates the skills people have. She views employees as interchangeable parts, regardless of skill set. Thus, she does not best use her staff, nor does she engender a positive working atmosphere."

"She should be more open to what others can do, and value their thoughts and ideas. People just don't speak up in meetings. If other ideas and thoughts are offered up, and she seems to not like them or disagrees, there seems to be no openness to finding out why, what, and how they think that way. She is so closed off to seeing other ways that can be explored."

8
DEVELOPMENT

More is expected of leaders today than at any point in modern business. Organizations move faster, and people are more autonomous than ever before. This pace will only quicken with time. Adaptive leaders keep up by pushing themselves and their people to sharpen the saw, acquire new skills, and evolve as the situation demands.

A major shortcoming of leaders who are static and do little more than maintain the status quo is their failure to develop their people. Too many leaders assume that developing your people is a manager's responsibility, and they let this important responsibility fall by the wayside as they move up the corporate ladder. You cannot expect your organization to operate at a high level if you do not equip your people to be their best. You are accountable as a leader for creating a culture where people stretch themselves to acquire new skills and abilities. You need to push people to be their best, just as you push yourself to do the same.

> **Too many leaders assume that developing your people is a manager's responsibility, and they let this important responsibility fall by the wayside as they move up the corporate ladder.**

Lifelong Learning

In many ways, leadership is a gift. The core leadership attributes we've explored are difficult to learn. More leaders are born with these skills than adopt them. However, these skills alone do not enable excellence, and this is where so many leaders fall short. They use the assumption that leadership skills are inherited to relieve themselves of any obligation to work on their leadership capabilities. The adaptive leader does not adhere to this rhetoric. The adaptive leader is a lifelong learner who is constantly looking for ways to improve his or her skills as well as develop new ones.

> **The adaptive leader is a lifelong learner who is constantly looking for ways to improve his or her skills as well as develop new ones.**

Lifelong learners don't peak. Their career trajectory maintains the same high arc that most experience only in their twenties and thirties. If leadership were a physical attribute, you would be limited by your age. Since it's a mental one, you can continue scaling new heights as long as you're willing to put in the work to get yourself to the top. The strategies that follow will help you get there.

1. Compete with Yourself

Competitive drive is your friend when it comes to lifelong learning. As long as you remain competitive and put yourself in challenging situations, you will have all the motivation you need to learn new things. Just as drive motivates you to be a lifelong learner, ego holds you back, and many leaders' insatiable drive is matched only by their ego. You cannot learn new skills without putting your ego in check. Your ego leaves you blind to your weaknesses and any opportunities for improvement. Ego prevents you from feeling vulnerable, and vulnerability is the key to stretching yourself and learning new skills. You cannot be a lifelong learner and blind to your weaknesses at the same time. Lifelong learners are willing to lean into their discomfort and look for ways they are falling short of their full potential. This is a competition in itself.

> **Just as drive motivates you to be a lifelong learner, ego holds you back, and many leaders' insatiable drive is matched only by their ego.**

2. Make Failure Your Classroom

Nothing will test your ability to be a lifelong learner like failure. Failure rips back the curtain on your weaknesses and exposes them to the world. Failure destroys the ego and puts you in a place where you have a simple choice—learn and press on or retreat and remain paralyzed. The choice sounds obvious, but for many who have risen to great heights professionally, it is far more comfortable to rest on their laurels and blame extraneous circumstances (the market, bad luck, etc.) for their misfortune. Adaptive leaders value failure. It removes your defenses and leaves you bare, which is immensely valuable because this shows you exactly where you need to head. No one likes to fail, but adaptive leaders recognize it for what it is—an opportunity to stretch yourself in brave new directions.

3. Read

Knowledge and inspiration drive personal innovation. You can get both from reading. Leaders often read voraciously early in their careers and lose this habit as they become established. Don't let this happen to you. Pick something to read that will challenge your thinking and expand your skill set. Keep this going, and you will remain informed and inspired.

> **Knowledge and inspiration drive personal innovation.**

4. Create a Stretch Assignment

Depending upon your responsibilities, you may not be able to literally leave your post and take a true stretch assignment (though you should if the opportunity exists). Instead, you can stretch your skills by spending time with someone who has vast knowledge of an area of the business you are unfamiliar with. Schedule regular meetings in which you aim to do nothing more than stretch your knowledge in new directions. People love to teach, and it won't take you long to find a great tutor.

5. Remain Humble

You have to be humble to exercise the skill of lifelong learning. Success breeds arrogance in ways that can be hard to see. If your skills as a leader are proven, it can be highly uncomfortable to admit you still have room for improvement. Many leaders don't continue to learn as they should because they associate this with what one is supposed to experience early in one's career. These leaders hold the expectation that their success lies in being decisive, confident, even cocksure. The great ones know this belief closes the door to self-improvement, and they remain humble.

> **Success breeds arrogance in ways that can be hard to see.**

6. Collect Quality Feedback

In some cases, your desire to learn will speak for itself. In others, failure will reveal gaps that must be filled. Most of the time, what you should or could learn is less apparent. This is a problem that's best solved with feedback. If you ask colleagues what they think you can improve, they will sense any defensiveness and resist disclosing the truth to save your feelings. If they report to you, they'll resist being honest to save their necks. You'll feel comfortable receiving this feedback, but you won't improve.

> **If you ask colleagues what they think you can improve, they will sense any defensiveness and resist disclosing the truth to save your feelings. If they report to you, they'll resist being honest to save their necks.**

A more effective option for obtaining quality feedback is to activate the complete 360° Refined™ assessment that came with this book. You can use it to send the same assessment that you took to the people you work with, only they will answer the questions about you. The results are anonymous (you can see data only aggregated by groups such as peers, direct reports, and customers), which motivates people to be completely honest in their evaluation of you. Your results pinpoint your leadership strengths and uncover opportunities to improve your leadership skills by revealing the specific skills from this book that you need to work on most. The open-ended questions give people the opportunity to elaborate on their feedback, share specific examples to broaden your understanding, and address any important areas that weren't measured by the assessment.

Whether you're seeking feedback in person or via the 360° Refined™ assessment, the process will inevitably test your tolerance for feeling vulnerable. In some places, the feedback will confirm things you're already aware of, positive and negative. In others, you may be introduced to a new Achilles' heel. With 360° Refined™, this is revealed in the accuracy chart. The accuracy chart uses self/other score comparisons to show where you've overestimated your skills, where you've rated your skills accurately, and where you've underestimated your skills. The larger the gap between what you and others see, the more critical it is you work to understand it.

> **In some places, the feedback will confirm things you're already aware of, positive and negative. In others, you may be introduced to a new Achilles' heel.**

When you review your feedback for the first time, try to absorb the message your colleagues are sending you.

Remember that your feedback is just data summarizing people's perceptions. These perceptions, right or wrong, reveal how people experience your leadership. These perceptions do not reflect your intentions or potential as a leader. You're the one who will decide your fate, and you'll be able to take the best path forward if you give your feedback careful consideration.

Adaptive leaders are constantly looking for innovative ways to expand the boundaries of their leadership effectiveness. Becoming a lifelong learner is a surefire way to increase your leadership skill set now and throughout your career.

What Lifelong Learning Looks Like

Lisa Marie A.
Lifelong learning score = 5.5*

What people who work with her say:

"She understands all the small parts and dependencies that make up a complete and successful solution. Once the solution is found, she doesn't stop. Lisa Marie constantly pushes herself to learn more, and finds ways to make our company even more successful based on what she discovers."

"Lisa Marie is open to new challenges and takes a 'dive right in' approach. She doesn't shy away from asking questions and stretching her skills. You'd think someone with her experience would rest on her laurels, but she continues to welcome new input and embrace learning opportunities."

"Lisa Marie strives to take on complex goals that move her out of her comfort zone. She is continually looking for ways to grow, especially on a professional level. She quickly learns the ins and outs of the challenge. She then immediately looks for ways she can ready the various functions to face the challenge along with her."

* Scores are on the 1- to 6-point scale (1=never and 6=always) from the 360° Refined™ test. Scores represent the average rating received from all who rated the executive. Scores and coworker comments are from actual people, though names and other identifying information have been altered.

William G.
Lifelong learning score = 5.7

What people who work with him say:

"When William does not know an issue, he strives to learn more about it by asking questions, reading background information, and diving deep into the issue. He loves his job and exudes excitement about what he is doing. It is often contagious. I often find he is very good even when he knows less about an issue because he approaches it with new angles and insights."

"Bill clearly spends time researching and learning about the industry and business on all levels. He is great at pushing himself to new heights. He has a natural aptitude for quickly learning."

"William is constantly learning and looking to absorb knowledge from every aspect of his position. He wants to know more about his profession and improve his skills."

What a Lack of Lifelong Learning Looks Like

Robby R.
Lifelong learning score = 1.3

What people who work with him say:

"Robby should admit what he doesn't know and be open to learn more about it, as opposed to delegating it to someone else. Basically, he needs to do his homework and show some effort. He's been here for a long time now. He should show more progress as a leader."

"Robby should be more willing to learn about himself and what he can do to improve. He should become a better listener and be more proactive about his professional development."

"Robby does not recognize that he is in a position where things change. No one expects him to know everything. Besides, he has never done some of these things before, but he needs to show some initiative to learn. He shouldn't resist coaching from many people; it will make him a better leader and will broaden his approach."

Thuy N.
Lifelong learning score = 2

What people who work with her say:

"Thuy needs to be more open minded about learning. Most important opportunities here require the ability to think differently. Therefore, she needs to let her guard down and be open to discovering something new. She can grow exponentially by opening herself up to these opportunities."

"Thuy doesn't have the initiative to learn. She asks other people to handle things that are really her area, and then when they show her how to do it herself, she doesn't pay attention. She ends up taking more of their time because they have to keep showing her over and over again."

"Thuy should take time to learn from her department managers instead of just telling them what she wants. It's a risk, in my opinion, to come into an organization thinking that you're already done learning everything you need to know."

Developing Others

It's striking how traditional notions of leadership continue to survive into this century. One that will limit you and everyone around you goes like this—*developing others is not a leader's responsibility*. A leader stuck in this outdated mode of thinking will turn up his or her nose at the idea of developing others, because it reeks of being "managerial" or a colossal waste of time. Fear not, for leaders who think this way will never provide much competition. Leaders who fail to develop others do not achieve excellence. They surround themselves with weak players and devote all their time and energy to themselves, to the detriment of their team. Leaders who fail to develop others weaken the organization.

> A leader stuck in this outdated mode of thinking will turn up his or her nose at the idea of developing others, because it reeks of being "managerial" or a colossal waste of time. Fear not, for leaders who think this way will never provide much competition.

Helping your people take their skills to a higher level creates a synergy that yields exponential results. Deepening your people's technical know-how and improving their weaknesses are essential to developing others. You also need to develop people's strengths and shape their perspectives about setbacks. The strategies that follow will show you how to pull this off.

1. Frame Your Intent, Then Stretch 'Em

Most of your people are going to react favorably to your efforts if you properly frame your desire to help them improve. People have to see and believe that your focus will be on them. Let your people know that you are looking to help them advance their careers by fully capitalizing on their strengths and stretching their knowledge and skills. Then offer projects and assignments that will do just that. This includes allowing room to fail along the way and following through with support when failures happen. It's not enough to say, "Mistakes are a good learning experience." You have

> **Let your people know that you are looking to help them advance their careers by fully capitalizing on their strengths and stretching their knowledge and skills.**

to back that statement up. Step in quickly after your employees make a mistake to help them explore what led to the mistake, what the consequences were, and what they would do differently next time.

2. Make Failure a Safe Word

Most people feel vulnerable after blowing it, and that vulnerability creates a fragile moment when real development can occur. Without your intervention, the moment will surface and vanish. When someone feels embarrassed, threatened, or incompetent, he or she is bound to get defensive, and this can block any real learning. Don't rush the conversation; you need to make it safe for them to talk. Your goal for the conversation should be mutual problem solving. Resist the urge to push for a commitment that they won't make the same mistake again; a development conversation is not the right time for this. Focus the conversation on analysis and understanding. The more you can get your staff to reveal what they were thinking and why they did what they did, the more data you have for helping them self-correct. A little humor can help calm their fears and open your employees up to discussing everything that led up to the mistake.

3. Shape How People Think

In the skilled hands of an adaptive leader, a vulnerable moment is valuable. It offers the opportunity to shape and mold the way an employee thinks. One person may need to reframe her negative thinking about the people she works with. Another may need to let go of the belief that he bothers you when he asks questions. Still another may stress herself out with self-defeating worries. All you

> **In the skilled hands of an adaptive leader, a vulnerable moment is valuable.**

have to do is discover the crutch, provide alternatives for them to try, and give them time and space to practice.

4. Reveal Your Failures

Many employees assume leaders land in their positions because they never mess up. Don't be shocked when you see surprise on a high potential's face whom you've told that you've made the same mistake in your career. Think of your memories as a great reference tool that you willingly hand over to those you lead.

5. Be a Coach

Your people's skills will truly blossom if you can take on the role of a coach. Acting as a coach means you focus on asking, rather than telling. It's tempting (for efficiency's sake) to tell people what to do so they can get it right and move on, but people don't learn anything from this (and it doesn't bolster their confidence). Asking people what they are going to do and how they are going to do it enables you to solve the problem together. This shows respect for their ideas and opinions, and makes it abundantly clear that their development is a high priority for you.

6. Set Goals

Goals are a great way to help your people go all the way in developing new skills. The conversations you have as a result of strategies one through five will lay the groundwork, and setting specific goals with your people will drive the effort home. People need to know what they are after. Having people set development goals that are written down and monitored gives them something tangible to pursue. If you hold your people accountable for reaching these goals (and provide guidance and support every step of the way), they will surprise you with how they are able to stretch and grow.

> **Having people set development goals that are written down and monitored gives them something tangible to pursue.**

Working with your people to develop their skills will set the expectation that this is how everyone should approach the work at hand. Staff will become more open, discovering new alternatives and broadening their mindsets. In addition to the technical know-how acquired along the way, these strategies build agile professionals.

What Developing Others Looks Like

Camille F.
Developing others score = 5.7*

What people who work with her say:
"Camille is highly sensitive to the growth of her management team. She spends a large amount of time mentoring them and ensuring each is gaining the skills necessary to be well rounded and diverse, and will be prepared to perform several roles and assignments across the company. I wish more of our executives would make this a priority."

"Camille is great at encouraging her managers to test their skills in new areas. She assigns projects appropriately and takes the time every few months to meet with each to discuss career goals, concerns, issues, etc. She is also very approachable, which makes it easy to go to her with questions or concerns."

"Nurturing the growth and development of someone is one of Camille's great talents. Whenever a decision is made in terms of cross-training or moving managers within our organization, a priority in her consideration is

* Scores are on the 1- to 6-point scale (1=never and 6=always) from the 360° Refined™ test. Scores represent the average rating received from all who rated the executive. Scores and coworker comments are from actual people, though names and other identifying information have been altered.

whether the decision will benefit the person's professional development. Personally, I've seen instances when Camille made decisions that took someone's career interest into account. I definitely think she takes the long-term view, and it benefits the company and the person."

Douglas F.
Developing others score = 6

What people who work with him say:
"Douglas has a natural gift for finding what people do best and supporting, praising, and encouraging that. He also points out weaknesses and shortcomings in a way that doesn't diminish or demean a person, but challenges them to greater accomplishments. He inspires a desire to overcome and master developmental needs. In the same vein, he uses people's strengths and needs to place them strategically in the best situations or positions for themselves and the company. The best examples that come to mind are his meaningful and effective performance reviews and how he makes a strong case for specific placements or changes when organizational revision is necessary."

"Douglas is a wonderful mentor, supervisor, and leader. He sincerely cares about my development (and others) and works closely with me after the project's end to provide a perspective on things to consider in the future."

"He is able to deliver feedback that is constructive and action oriented to his staff and to clients. Even if the feedback is not completely positive, he delivers it in such a compassionate way that the person hears it and isn't defensive."

What a Lack of Developing Others Looks Like

Pam T.
Developing others score = 1.3

What people who work with her say:
"It would be nice to have opportunities to develop skills and talents to prepare us for opportunities beyond this department. I wish she would teach some of the things she knows to the people below her to broaden their knowledge base."

"Across Pam's department, people are not being groomed for new challenges. Employee development is lost to the tyranny of next quarter's, or next year's, business pressures. It gives people precious little time to develop themselves so they can be better for the organization in the future."

"Pam tends to not address the developmental needs of her staff. Often, people do not know what areas they need to improve in, in order to grow in the organization. She should provide a suggested growth plan to individuals. She should also let someone know when she feels there is no plan to promote."

Evan P.
Developing others score = 2.3

What people who work with him say:

"What's holding Evan back is how little time he invests in his team. He focuses on day-to-day tasks, and does not see the big picture or each associate's development needs. He should take a fresh look and focus on building a great and talented team."

"Evan has been spending too much time micromanaging and doesn't allow associates to make mistakes. He needs to trust the team so they can develop self-reliance and accountability. It is their job to make sure they stay on top of their tasks. His role as coach should be a more supportive role. He should be available for guidance when needed. Right now he rarely gives feedback regarding most situations."

"I wish Evan would focus on developing his people ahead of himself. He has had good people on his team for a number of years. However, they tell me they do not feel as though their professional development is supported every day. They believe they come in a distant third to getting the job done, and to Evan getting credit. He has to focus on developing the team that supports his success."

<u>APPENDIX A</u>
The Research Behind 360°
Refined™

I t's our business to discover what qualities propel successful people, so that anyone can apply these skills to their benefit. Numbers are powerful, but they only tell half the truth. In the end, they are only as powerful as the lives they touch.

360° Refined™ is held to the strictest standards for research in its design and validation. The assessment items were developed, validated, and tested over a decade in a host of organizations of varying sizes. More than 70,000 leaders have taken 360° Refined™, and this massive normative database yields outstanding validity data to support the assessment.

The 75 items that make up the closed-ended questions in 360° Refined™ were written as behavioral impact statements, a proprietary method of creating assessments that are brief and highly accurate. The behavioral impact method enables an assessment to measure a broader range of skills in a shorter period of time, increasing the accuracy of a participant's responding by both taking the focus away from responses that are right or wrong, and by keeping their attention while they are taking the test.

Creating behavioral impact statements involves an iterative process of writing draft questions and reworking them to fit what is necessary and sufficient (no more and no less than what covers the elements of that skill) to assess each competency. This proprietary method of drafting survey questions eliminates unnecessary questions by avoiding the practice of using many specific behavioral questions to attempt to measure a single skill. Instead, the test questions measure the sufficient behavioral outcome needed to adequately assess a particular skill. For example, the competency titled "communication" does not ask questions about every specific method of communication that a leader may use in the workplace. Rather, it assesses the impact of a leader's ability to communicate by measuring coworkers' reactions to the leader's communicative behaviors.

The survey questions used in the assessment describe critical aspects of each of the 22 leadership skills through the typical behavior of the individual being assessed. The frequency with which an individual demonstrates behaviors related to a skill are the best measure of that skill. Therefore, the test questions are structured using a six-point frequency scale, which narrows in on the frequency with which the individual demonstrates the behavior in question.

Statistical Validity

Statistical analyses are used to confirm the validity of the 360° Refined™ assessment. The first step in evaluating items in an assessment concerns the concept of face validity. Face validity pertains to whether the test questions appear to be a valid representation of the concept, so that observers and assessment examinees will accept the results. Once the survey questions met the face validity criteria, they were presented cold to additional subject matter experts for further confirmation. The subject matter experts included doctorate- and master-level industrial psychologists, as well as seasoned MBA-trained businesspeople with extensive executive-level experience.

The next step was to ascertain the reliability of the assessment. Reliability is a term used to describe the tendency for clusters of items to consistently measure an associated construct. Each of the 22 skills measured by 360° Refined™ generate a unique reliability score, which is measured using the Cronbach's Alpha statistic. Cronbach's Alpha ranges from 0.0 to 1.0. Target reliabilities should be greater than .70. The Cronbach's Alpha values for the 22 skills measured by 360° Refined™ ranged from .85-.95, which is considered a strong indication of the reliability of each skill measured by the assessment. The reliabilities measured for each of the 22 skills are listed in the table that follows.

Cronbach's Alpha Reliability Coefficients for the Skills Measured by 360° Refined™

Skill	Number of Items	Cronbach's Alpha
Self-Awareness	3	.85
Self-Management	3	.88
Social Awareness	3	.91
Relationship Management	3	.86
Risk Taking	4	.94
Planning	3	.93
Vision	3	.90
Courage to Lead	3	.92
Decision Making	3	.94
Communication	3	.93
Acumen	4	.88
Mobilizing Others	6	.90
Results Focus	4	.93
Information Sharing	3	.92
Outcome Concern	3	.87
Agility	4	.92
Integrity	3	.95
Credibility	3	.93
Values Differences	3	.92
Lifelong Learning	4	.92
Decision Fairness	4	.91
Developing Others	3	.92

Construct Validity

To assess the dimensionality of 360° Refined™, an exploratory factor analysis was performed on the 75 items. The Kaiser-Meyer-Oklin value was .944, exceeding the recommended value of .6. The Bartlett's Test of Sphericity reached statistical significance, which supports the factorability of the correlation matrix. A principal component analysis suggested a two-factor solution with the two factors accounting for 50.53% of the variance in the correlation matrix. A Catell's Scree Test provided further confirmation of the proposed two-factor structure with the plot of the eigenvalues breaking and becoming horizontal at or near two. The interpretation of the two factors is consistent with the design of the 360° Refined™ core and adaptive leadership superfactors. Taken with the reliability analysis already described, these results support the two-factor structure of 360° Refined™.

Comparison to Job Performance

The final, critical step compared scores on 360° Refined™ to leaders' on-the-job performance. Multiple regression was the statistical technique used to make this comparison. Leaders' self-evaluations were limited in accounting for their job performance with these scores explaining just 12.2% of the variance in their job performance. Ratings from coworkers were highly significant (at the .000 level) in explaining leaders' job performance. Ratings from coworkers explained 43.2% of the variance in leaders' job performance.

Appendix B

Discussion Questions for Reading Groups

Getting a group together to discuss Leadership 2.0 will help you bridge the learning-doing gap. Use the following questions to start a meaningful conversation and build your understanding of the core and adaptive leadership skills.

1. What is the most important thing you discovered while reading Leadership 2.0?

2. What is your position on the relative importance of the core and adaptive leadership skills?

3. Which skills stood out to you? Do you think most leaders fall short in any particular skill?

4. What fundamental changes would you like to make to your leadership style now that you know about the core and adaptive leadership skills?

5. Does anyone in the group have a vision statement they'd like to polish? Have them share it with the group to test it against the recommendations suggested in the strategy chapter.

6. Among the core leadership skills, which do group members struggle with the most? Share your challenges and discuss them together.

7. Among the adaptive leadership skills, which do group members struggle with the most? Share your challenges and discuss them together.

8. Is there anything covered in the book that you will take action on in the next quarter? How about in the next week?

9. Who in the group was already familiar with emotional intelligence? To whom was it new?

10. Which emotional intelligence strategies will you add to your leadership approach?

11. How do you see emotional intelligence in action among the leaders in your organization?

12. Had anyone heard of organizational justice before reading this book? What do you know about it?

13. How do you see organizational justice in action among the leaders in your organization?

14. What challenges or dilemmas have tested your character in your career so far? What do you think you did or didn't do well now that you reflect on it?

15. Who have been your leadership heroes or role models?

16. Which historical figures were influenced by poor leadership or great leadership? Which leadership skills helped them succeed or fail?

17. How are these leadership skills (strategy, action, results, emotional intelligence, organizational justice, character, and development) visible in current events today? Discuss politicians, celebrities, athletes, and business leaders in the news.

18. For groups who decide to take the 360° Refined™ assessment before meeting, you can bring your results to the meeting and discuss them as follows:

    a. Without sharing specific numbers, which leadership skills were your highest?

    b. Were your highest scores much higher than the others, or were they relatively close?

    c. Which leadership skill was your lowest? Which strategies will you employ to improve this skill?

19. What will make practicing your leadership skills challenging? What ideas or advice do group members have to offer?

20. Which lessons from the book should be taught to future leaders?

LEARN MORE

The authors are the cofounders of TalentSmart®, a global consultancy that serves more than 75% of Fortune 500 companies and is the world's leading provider of emotional intelligence tests and training.

TalentSmart® offers free resources, including articles, whitepapers, and a newsletter covering the latest in workplace learning at:

www.TalentSmart.com/learn

If you'd like more information on 360° Refined™, including tips for getting the most from your 360°, visit:

www.TalentSmart.com/360

If you're interested in learning more about leadership, 360° feedback, or are looking for tools to assist you in teaching others, review the resources on the remaining pages and contact us at:

888.818.SMART
(toll free, US & Canada callers)

or

858.509.0582

Visit us on the web at: www.TalentSmart.com

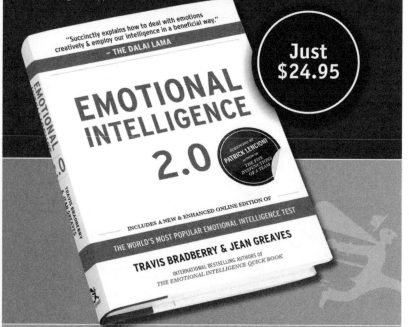

EMOTIONAL INTELLIGENCE 2.0

"This book can drastically change the way you think about success ... read it twice."

From the foreword by Patrick Lencioni, author of the blockbuster *The Five Dysfunctions of a Team*

WHAT PEOPLE ARE SAYING ABOUT THE BOOK:

"What distinguishes human beings is that we are capable of positive change. This book succinctly explains how to deal with emotions creatively and employ our intelligence in a beneficial way."
❧ **THE DALAI LAMA**

"A fast read with compelling anecdotes and good context in which to understand and improve your score."
❧ **NEWSWEEK**

"I distributed the book to my entire team. It's a wonderful tool that can change not only your professional career but also your personal relationships."
❧ **REGINA SACHA,** VP OF HR, FEDEX

"Research shows convincingly that EQ is more important than IQ. Gives abundant, practical findings and insights with emphasis on how to develop EQ."
❧ **STEPHEN R. COVEY,** AUTHOR, *The 7 Habits of Highly Effective People*

"This book is excellent, and the learning included with the free online test is cutting edge. I strongly recommend it."
❧ **KEN BLANCHARD,** COAUTHOR, *The One Minute Manager*

to order online, visit www.talentsmart.com or call 888.818.SMART

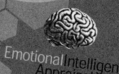

THE EMOTIONAL INTELLIGENCE APPRAISAL®

MULTI-RATER (360°) EDITION

- You control the administration.
- No waiting for results—you receive them instantly.
- Includes open-ended comments.
- Collects ratings from up to 26 of your peers, direct reports, supervisors, and others.

Online with e-learning for just $199.95

Volume, government, education, and non-profit discounts available

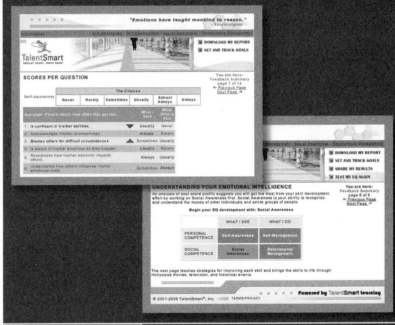

CONSULTANT EDITION

Our system sends the *Emotional Intelligence Appraisal® - Me Edition* to your participants and conceals their scores from them. Great for coaches and trainers needing to see participants' scores before they do. You can view participants' results from the administration page and forward their complete feedback reports to them at the time of your choosing.

Online with e-learning for just $49.95

Volume, government, education, and non-profit discounts available

to order online, visit www.talentsmart.com or call 888.818.SMART

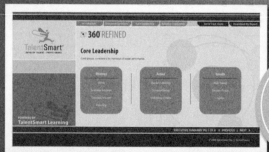

INNOVATION • CLARITY • EASE

Drill down from your five highest- and lowest-rated leadership skills followed by your five highest-
and lowest-rated behaviors.

Bar charts make it easy
to see how you rated
yourself compared to how:

1. Everyone rated you
2. Your peers rated you
3. Your supervisor or
   board rated you
4. Your staff rated you
5. Others rated you
   (a group you select)

Discover how self-aware you are by learning whether you tend to
overestimate, underestimate, or accurately estimate your skills
compared to how others see you.

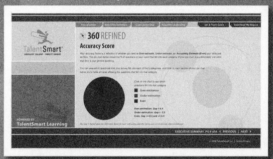

Click on each section of the pie chart (red, green, or blue) to find
the very behaviors and scores where you overrated, underrated, or
accurately rated yourself.

WHAT PEOPLE SAY ABOUT THE *360° REFINED* REPORT

- "Quickly narrows in on exactly which skills to develop."
- "The report layout offers both depth and scope of information."
- "It's powerful to see how the written comments from my staff connect
  so well with their ratings."

---

to order online, visit **www.talentsmart.com** or call **888.818.SMART**